Microwave Magic

Poultry

Grolier Limited
TORONTO

Contributors to this series:

Recipes and Technical Assistance:
École de cuisine Bachand-Bissonnette
Cooking consultants:
Michèle Emond, Denis Bissonnette
Photos:
Laramée Morel Communications
Audio-Visuelles
Design:
Claudette Taillefer
Assistants: Joan Pothier
          Julie Deslauriers
          Philippe O'Connor
Accessories: Andrée Cournoyer
Editing: Communications
          La Griffe Inc.

Assembly: Marc Vallières
          Vital Lapalme
          Carole Garon
          Jean-Pierre Larose
Production Manager:
Gilles Chamberland
Art Director:
Bernard Lamy
Consultants:
Roger Aubin
Joseph R. De Varennes
Gaston Lavoie
Jocelyn Smyth
Donna Thomson
Production:
Le Groupe Polygone Éditeurs Inc.

The series editors have taken every care to ensure that the information given is accurate. However, no cookbook can guarantee the user successful results. The editors cannot accept any responsibility for the results obtained by following the recipes and recommendations given.

Canadian Cataloguing in Publication Data

Poultry
(Microwave magic ; 2)
Translation of: La Volaille.
Includes index.
ISBN 0-7172-2376-0

1. Microwave cookery.   2. Cookery (Chicken).
I. Series: Microwave magic (Toronto, Ont.) ; 2.

TX832.C4813 1987   641.5'882   C87-094418-5

Table of Contents

Each of the twenty-six volumes is devoted to a particular type of cooking for ease of reference. So, if you are looking for chicken recipes, you simply go to one of the two volumes on that subject. Each volume has its own index, and the final volume will contain a general index to the complete series.

The series puts over one thousand two hundred recipes at your fingertips. You will find it as useful as the microwave oven itself. Enjoy!

Note from the Editor

How to Use this Book
The books in this set have been designed to make your job as easy as possible. As a result, most of the recipes are set out in a standard way.

We suggest that you begin by consulting the information chart for the recipe you have chosen. You will find there all the information you need to decide if you are able to make it: preparation time, cost per serving, level of difficulty, number of calories per serving and other relevant details. Thus, if you have only 30 minutes in which to prepare the evening meal, you will quickly be able to tell which recipe is possible and suits your schedule.

The list of ingredients is always clearly separated from the main text. When space allows, the ingredients are shown together in a photograph so that you can make sure you have them all without rereading the list—

another way of saving your valuable time. In addition, for the more complex recipes we have supplied photographs of the key stages involved either in preparation or serving.

All the dishes in this book have been cooked in a 700 watt microwave oven. If your oven has a different wattage, consult the conversion chart that appears on the following page for cooking times in different types of oven. We would like to emphasize that the cooking times given in the book are a minimum. If a dish does not seem to be cooked enough, you may return it to the oven for a few more minutes. Also, the cooking time can vary according to your ingredients: their water and fat content, thickness, shape and even where they come from. We have therefore left a blank space on each recipe page in which you can note

the cooking time that suits you best. This will enable you to add a personal touch to the recipes that we suggest and to reproduce your best results every time.

Although we have put all the technical information together at the front of this book, we have inserted a number of boxed entries called **MICROTIPS** through-out to explain particular techniques. They are brief and simple, and will help you obtain successful results in your cooking.

With the very first recipe you try, you will discover just how simple microwave cooking can be and how often it depends on techniques you already use for cooking with a conventional oven. If cooking is a pleasure for you, as it is for us, it will be all the more so with a microwave oven. Now let's get on with the food.

The Editor

Key to the Symbols
For ease of reference, the following symbols have been used on the recipe information charts.

The pencil symbol ✏ is a reminder to write your cooking time in the space provided.

Level of Difficulty

🍴 Easy

🍴🍴 Moderate

🍴🍴🍴 Complex

Cost per Serving

$ Inexpensive

$$ Moderate

$$$ Expensive

Power Levels

All the recipes in this book have been tested in a 700 watt oven. As there are many microwave ovens on the market with different power levels, and as the names of these levels vary from one manufacturer to another, we have decided to give power levels as a percentage. To adapt the power levels given here, consult the chart opposite and the instruction manual for your oven.

Generally speaking, if you have a 500 watt or 600 watt oven you should increase cooking times by about 30% over those given, depending on the actual length of time required. The shorter the original cooking time, the greater the percentage by which it must be lengthened. The 30% figure is only an average. Consult the chart for detailed information on this topic.

Power Levels

HIGH: 100% - 90%	Vegetables (except boiled potatoes and carrots) Soup Sauce Fruits Browning ground beef Browning dish Popcorn
MEDIUM HIGH: 80% - 70%	Rapid defrosting of precooked dishes Muffins Some cakes Hot dogs
MEDIUM: 60% - 50%	Cooking tender meat Cakes Fish Seafood Eggs Reheating Boiled potatoes and carrots
MEDIUM LOW: 40%	Cooking less tender meat Simmering Melting chocolate
DEFROST: 30% **LOW: 30% - 20%**	Defrosting Simmering Cooking less tender meat
WARM: 10%	Keeping food warm Allowing yeast dough to rise

Cooking Time Conversion Chart

700 watts	600 watts*
5 s	11 s
15 s	20 s
30 s	40 s
45 s	1 min
1 min	1 min 20 s
2 min	2 min 40 s
3 min	4 min
4 min	5 min 20 s
5 min	6 min 40 s
6 min	8 min
7 min	9 min 20 s
8 min	10 min 40 s
9 min	12 min
10 min	13 min 30 s
20 min	26 min 40 s
30 min	40 min
40 min	53 min 40 s
50 min	66 min 40 s
1 h	1 h 20 min

* There is very little difference in cooking times between 500 watt ovens and 600 watt ovens.

Poultry

Poultry provides one of the world's favorite meats. Of the various types of fowl available, chicken is by far the most popular, and people in countries throughout the world have long enjoyed its tender, juicy meat.

Chicken is served in every culture, and the ways of cooking it vary accordingly. For example, chicken is used in Arab couscous, Austrian *Backhuhn,* Flemish *waterzooi,* Italian *pollo alla diavola,* Georgian *chakhokhbili,* Indian *tandoori,* Malaysian *satay,* Moroccan *bastelah,* Japanese *oyako donburi* and many other national dishes. Closer to home, the culinary traditions of France offer a thousand and one ways of preparing it: boiled, braised, roasted, fried, grilled; in pâtés, soups and fricassées; hot or cold; whole or in pieces; with or without sauce. As you can see, the ways of cooking chicken are infinite.

However, the universal popularity of chicken should not make us forget other types of poultry. Many other types are available and their taste is often on a par with that of chicken. Turkey is certainly the best known alternative. Its large size and its lean, juicy flesh make it the ideal bird to serve when there are many guests, and it is frequently selected for this purpose by home cooks and professional caterers alike.

Next comes duck, which French cooks frequently transform with an orange sauce. Although it has more bone and fat than chicken it is universally prized, particularly in Chinese cooking. Alessandro Filippini, a distinguished chef at America's famous Delmonico restaurant, called it the king of the birds. Strictly speaking, the term ''duck'' is applied to birds that are more than two months old. Younger birds are called ducklings, and they have even finer meat. If you are able to choose the way in which the bird is to be slaughtered, request strangulation rather than decapitation; this method allows the blood to remain distributed throughout the meat, making it redder and juicier and giving it a faintly gamey taste.

People who like fatty meat will enjoy goose. Although rarely served in Canadian homes, it has much to offer those who enjoy new taste experiences.

Game is closely associated with poultry. Young partridges are hunted for their juicy flesh, which has a delicious wild flavor. Then there is pheasant, the lean flesh of which is the perfect foil for rich, fragrant sauces. Quails, on the other hand, have a more delicate taste and are prized because, being small, they are elegant to serve.

How to Joint a Chicken

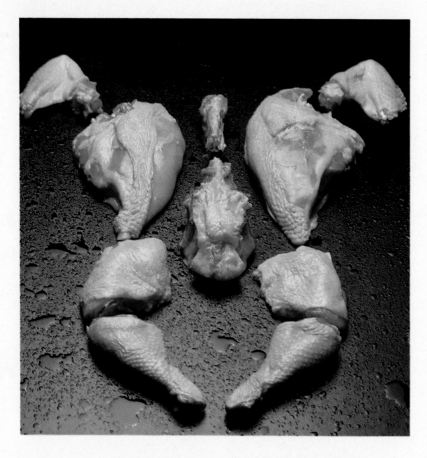

Knowing how to joint a chicken can save you money. Also, whole chickens are often higher in quality than those that are sold in parts. Mastering the technique of cutting a chicken into pieces can increase your enjoyment of cooking.

with the legs, which include the drumstick and the thigh. Cut the legs off first and divide each one into two separate pieces, then remove the wings. You are then able to cut through the rib cage so as to separate the breast from the back. The back can be cut, across the backbone, to yield two pieces. Finally, cut the breast lengthwise into halves. You will then have ten neatly cut pieces and no waste. On pages 12 and 13 another method, yielding pieces more equivalent in size but few in number, is described.

Once the chicken is jointed those parts not immediately required can be frozen and, when needed, quickly thawed in the microwave. By jointing a few birds, you can have a good supply of chicken pieces on hand to use in the recipes given in this book.

Although you can buy chicken in pieces in supermarkets, we recommend that you buy whole birds. In many cases they are higher in quality and they are usually much less expensive. Also, if you joint the bird yourself you will have neater pieces and you will have the giblets to use. It is very easy to joint a chicken if you go about it methodically, step by step. The only tools you need are a cutting board and a good quality knife with a very sharp, pointed blade. The rest depends on skill.

Although the illustrations here show a chicken, the basic principles for jointing a bird can be applied to other fowl, such as turkey, duck or pheasant.

Any technique has its own particular method. The one we have chosen here begins

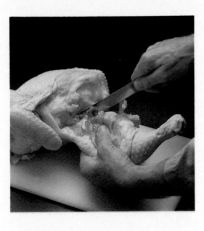

1. Removing the Legs
Begin by laying the chicken on its back. Carefully pull one leg outwards and cut into it at the point where the thigh joins the hip. If the ball-and-socket joint between the thigh and hip bones does not separate, bend the thigh downwards to break it. Complete the procedure by cutting neatly through the joint. Repeat the entire step for the other leg.

2. Separating the Drumstick from the Thigh
Place each leg on the cutting board skin side down and cut through the joint between the drumstick and thigh. It is not worth making this cut if the legs are very small.

3. Removing the Wings
Use gentle pressure to hold the wing against the body of the chicken in order to feel the shoulder ball-and-socket joint. Make a cut in the hollow of the joint, pull the wing outwards and cut the skin at the base of the wing. Repeat for the other wing.

4. Dividing the Carcass
Place the knife in the cavity at the tail end of the carcass and cut alongside the backbone to the rib cage. Then cut through the rib cage by pulling the knife toward you and keeping the blade parallel to the backbone. Repeat for the other side.

5. Removing the Back
You can now separate the breast from the back, pulling them apart so as to free the shoulder bones and cutting through them. Cut across the backbone where the rib cage ends to obtain two separate pieces.

6. Dividing the Breast
To cut the breast in two place it on the board skin side down. Then cut down the length of the breastbone (the prominent central bone to which the meat is attached), splitting the breast by putting pressure on the knife to either the left or right of the bone. When dealing with a large turkey or goose, cut each breast across as well to obtain four or even six pieces.

Cutting a Bird into Equal Sized Pieces

To obtain pieces of roughly equal size, begin by loosening the meat adjoining the parson's nose (the oysters) and removing the legs but leaving the thighs and drumsticks attached. Separate the back from the breast and then remove the wings so that the wing portion includes some of the breast meat. This method yields five rather than ten pieces.

The cutting method described on pages 10 and 11 has the double advantage of being quick and economical. However, professional cooks and butchers use another method to obtain larger pieces, of roughly equal size.

In this method the legs are first removed but the drumsticks and thighs are not separated. Each leg is cut off in a single piece, along with the oysters, which have already been detached from the carcass. The bony end of the drumstick is then removed.

The breast, with wings attached, is then separated from the back, as outlined on page 13.

Then the wings proper are removed, with some of the tender white breast meat, yielding larger, meatier pieces than would each wing alone. Note that the wing tips, having very little meat, are removed and can be used to make stock.

MICROTIPS

For Perfect Pastry Shells in the Microwave Oven

You can make crisp and flaky pastry shells quickly and easily in your microwave. Roll out the pastry in the usual way and line a pie plate with it. Prick the base with a fork and cover it with dried peas before putting it in the oven to prevent the pastry from rising or shrinking away from the edges of the pan. Cook for approximately 6 minutes at 70%.

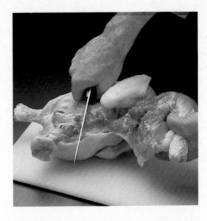

1. Removing the Legs
To deal with the legs, turn the chicken onto its back. Insert the blade of your knife at the point where the thigh joins the body and cut through the skin. Then pull the thigh outwards to free the bone at the joint. Cut through the joint itself, taking care that the wedge of flesh freed from the carcass in step 2 remains attached to the thigh. Finally, remove the bony end of the drumstick and make a nick in the large tendon joining the drumstick to the thigh to prevent the leg from losing its shape during cooking. Repeat for the other leg.

2. Removing the Oysters
These wedges of flesh, adjoining the parson's nose and extending into the hollow on each side of the backbone, are frequently overlooked. Free them from the carcass, using the point of the knife, but do not cut through the skin that covers them and keeps them attached to the thigh.

3. Freeing the Legs
To finish freeing the legs from the body, simply make one cut along the backbone and a second one below the shoulder blade.

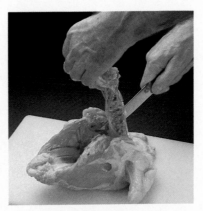

4. Freeing the Shoulders
Turn the chicken over, onto its breast again. Place the knife between the backbone and one of the shoulder blades. Using a fair amount of pressure, cut through the flesh to the cavity. Leave the wing attached to the breast. Repeat for the other side of the backbone.

5. Removing the Back
Insert the knife into the cavity of the bird and cut into one side between the shoulder and the rib cage. Cut along the rib cage parallel to the backbone. Do the same on the other side. The back will come away easily because you have already freed the shoulders.

6. Removing the Wings
After removing the back, turn the breast skin side up. Pull the wings away from the body and chop off the tips. Working diagonally so that the wing portion includes some of the white breast meat, cut through the point where the collarbone joins the breastbone. Repeat for the other wing.

Boning Poultry

Boning the Breast

1. Lay the breast on the cutting board, skin side up. Place the palm of the hand on the breast and press down hard so as to break the breastbone, separating it from the ribs and making it easier to remove.

2. Turn the breast over and, using your fingers, pry the breastbone from the thick part of the flesh. It will come away easily as it has already been dislodged. Using a knife or your fingers, carefully lift the flesh off the ribs, which are visible on the inner surface.

3. Finally, pry the remaining piece of cartilage off with your thumb tips. It will pull away from the flesh quite easily. Check for any small bones that remain and remove them. You will be left with a complete breast, free of bone and cartilage.

MICROTIPS

Preparing Poultry for Cooking

Here are some practical tips to help you cook poultry successfully.

Because the skin is the fattiest part of the bird, removing it will result in meals that have less fat and are lower in calories.

If the bird is to be stuffed, be sure that the stuffing is quite cold and that it is stuffed just prior to cooking. These precautions prevent the growth of bacteria.

If you are concerned about the appearance of the bird for serving, truss it before cooking. The original shape of the bird will then be retained.

Boning the Legs

1. The technique shown here enables you to bone the leg without cutting into the flesh. This technique is very useful for stuffing the legs because tying them is then unnecessary. Hold the drumstick firmly in one hand and scrape the top of the thighbone (femur) with the blade of the knife to remove the thin membrane holding the flesh to the bone. Once the top of this bone is free pull on it, separating it from the lower legbone, called the tibia.

2. Once the thighbone has been removed, scrape the kneecap and the tibia in the same way. Although the meat in the illustration appears to have lost its shape, it will return to its original shape when all the bones are out.

3. When the tibia is well scraped, pull on it. It will come away with little effort. Reshape the leg and, if desired, fill it with stuffing.

To enhance the flavor of a turkey or a chicken, we recommend that you brush it with a sauce containing the seasonings preferred by you. Use sweet, unsalted butter in the sauce so that the skin will not harden or crack.

Be sure to raise the chicken slightly above the level of the cooking dish, perhaps by placing it on an overturned saucer, so that the fat can drain into the dish. It is also a good idea to put a toothpick between the dish and the saucer to prevent their sticking together by suction, which would make the saucer difficult to remove.

Cooked chicken pieces can be used at a later date. For example, drumsticks can be kept frozen for four months. They will be just as crisp and tasty when you defrost them in the microwave oven.

Freezing Poultry

Poultry can be kept for up to six months in the freezer if it is properly wrapped to protect it from the cold, dry air. When it comes to wrappings, freezer bags that can be hermetically sealed are a good investment; they keep poultry and other meats well protected in the freezer.

protected by covering them with aluminum foil before freezing (see page 17). The bird (either whole or in pieces) should then be placed in a hermetically sealed bag to protect the meat from the cold, dry air and to help retain the flavor.

If you do not have a sealing device, freezer bags with tie fastenings or special-purpose containers may be used. Be sure to label each container to indicate its contents and the date it was put in the freezer.

If you do not want to freeze your chicken, it is best to cook it the day you buy it. If it is to be cooked on the following day, remove its wrapping, wash and dry it and wrap it in plastic film. Fresh turkey or turkey pieces can be kept in the refrigerator in their original wrapping for up to two days.

Although a number of cooks claim that frozen birds have less flavor than fresh, freezing is still a satisfactory way to preserve most types of poultry, whole birds and individual pieces alike. A fresh bird can be kept for about six months in the freezer. Note, however, that the giblets should be wrapped separately and used within three months. If you buy a frozen bird, check the package for softness and make sure that it does not contain any pinkish ice. Either condition means that the bird has been accidentally defrosted and then refrozen.

If you buy a fresh bird to freeze, remove its original wrapping. If it is likely that the bird will be defrosted and cooked in the microwave, the thinner parts can be

Defrosting Poultry

1. Take the bird out of the freezer and place it, in its wrapping, breast side up on a rack.

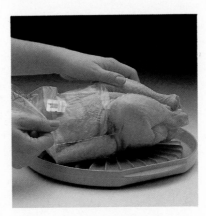

2. Remove the wrapping. Check that all parts of the bird are still fully frozen. Protect any partially thawed parts by covering them with aluminum foil.

3. Before placing the bird in the microwave oven, use aluminum foil to shield the thinner parts (the ends of the legs, the wing tips and the ridge of the breast along the breastbone). The foil will prevent these parts from beginning to cook and allow for more even defrosting.

4. Divide the total time required for defrosting the bird in the microwave oven into short periods and allow for standing times of about a quarter of the total defrosting time between each. Halfway through the defrosting time, give the dish a half-turn so that the microwave energy is more evenly distributed over all parts of the bird.

5. At the same time turn the bird and lay it breast side down on the dish so that the back is more exposed to the microwaves. This step also prevents the breast from beginning to cook prematurely.

6. At the end of the total defrost time, remove the bird from the oven. Remove the giblets as well and allow to stand. This standing time is needed for thorough and even defrosting.

Defrosting the Legs

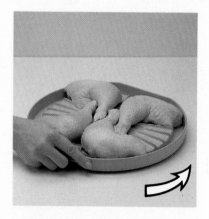

1. Frozen legs bought at the supermarket frequently come stuck together in a single block, making it impossible to separate them before thawing. In such cases, put them on a bacon rack in the microwave oven at the appropriate power level for defrosting. After 6 to 8 minutes, check to see whether they are sufficiently thawed to be separated. If not, continue to check every 2 minutes until they are.

2. Arrange the legs in a circle, taking care to place the thicker parts toward the outside of the dish. Divide the total time they require in the microwave into periods of equal length and allow for standing times of a quarter of the total defrosting time between each.

3. Halfway through the defrosting process, give the dish a half-turn so as to ensure even defrosting. Once the defrosting time is up, take the legs out of the oven and allow them to stand for 10 minutes. Rinse in cold water and pat dry before cooking.

MICROTIPS

Defrosting Chicken Breasts

To ensure that chicken breasts defrost evenly place them on a bacon rack, leaving equal space between each. Set the defrosting time and remember to divide it into periods of equal length in the microwave, with standing times of a quarter of the total defrosting time between each period. Halfway through the defrosting process, turn each breast so that the part that was near the outside of the dish is now on the inside. At the end of the time required in the microwave, remove the breasts from the oven and allow them to stand for 10 minutes. Rinse and pat dry before cooking.

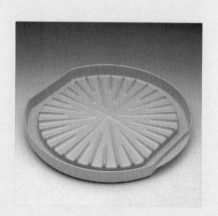

Defrosting Poultry
Power level: 30%

Type of Piece	Quantity	Defrosting Time	Standing Time*
Whole chicken		8 to 12 min/kg (4 to 6 min/lb)	10 to 20 min
Whole turkey		12 to 16 min/kg (6 to 8 min/lb)	30 to 60 min in cold water
Quarters	4 x 250 g (8 oz)	15 min	10 min
Wings	900 g (2 lb) 450 g (1 lb)	15 min 8 min	10 min 10 min
Drumsticks	6 x 125 g (4 oz)	12 min	10 min
Boneless breasts	4 x 250 g (8 oz) 2 x 250 g (8 oz)	15 min 8 min	10 min 10 min
Legs	8 x 125 g (4 oz) 4 x 125 g (4 oz)	15 min 8 min	10 min 10 min

* The time in the microwave must be alternated with standing times equal to a quarter of the total defrosting time. So, when dealing with poultry, there should be four periods in the microwave, each followed by a period of standing time. The standing time in this chart refers to that time required after the microwaving is complete.

MICROTIPS

Defrosting a Whole Bird

Although the defrosting technique described here refers to a chicken, it can be used for all types of poultry. We should mention that many experts claim that it is better to defrost poultry in the traditional way, that is, in the refrigerator. However, as this method can take up to four hours per kilogram (e.g., for a whole turkey) we believe it is more practical to speed up the process by using the microwave oven. Don't worry—your guests will enjoy the food just as much. To defrost a bird in the microwave, put it on a bacon rack (or some other type of rack) to keep it out of its juices, which seep out and absorb more microwaves than the meat. If the bird is allowed to stand in its own juices, those parts that are submerged will begin to cook in the hot liquid.

For a whole chicken, allow 10 to 12 minutes per kilo at 30% (the standard power level for defrosting). Drumsticks weighing 125 g each will defrost in 12 minutes or less. Consult the chart on this page for defrosting times.

Cooking Poultry

 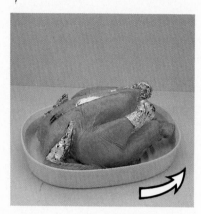 

1. To ensure even cooking and to avoid overcooking the thinner parts of a bird, cover the ends of the legs and the wing tips as well as the ridge of the breast along the breastbone with aluminum foil.

2. Halfway through the cooking time, give the dish a half-turn unless your oven is equipped with a turntable. This turn is necessary because the microwaves are not usually evenly distributed throughout the oven.

3. Three-quarters of the way through the cooking time, turn the bird breast side down on the dish. At the end of the cooking time given in the recipe, pierce the thigh with a fork. If the juice runs clear and the flesh shows signs of coming away, the bird is done. Allow it to stand for 10 minutes to allow the internal temperature to be evenly distributed.

Sauces and Seasonings Suitable for Browning Poultry

Ingredients	Instructions
Soy sauce or Teriyaki sauce	Brush
Barbecue sauce	Brush or pour over before serving
Melted butter and paprika	Brush with butter and sprinkle with paprika
Brown sauces and sweet sauces with melted butter	Brush
Honey, jams and jellies	Glaze before cooking or halfway through cooking time

Arranging Poultry

It is obvious that the proper way to arrange chicken pieces for cooking is the same as that for defrosting; the thicker parts should always face the outside of the dish. Also, the way in which the microwaves are distributed throughout the oven means that the cavity of a whole bird receives less heat than the other parts, which explains the necessity of changing the position of the bird halfway through the cooking time.

Cooking Bags for Use with Chicken

1. To boil a whole chicken (or chicken pieces intended for use in sandwiches or salads), use a cooking bag. Begin by washing and drying the chicken.

2. Put the chicken into the bag and add a cup of liquid. Fasten the bag loosely with a plastic tie

or punch a few holes in it so that the steam can escape.

3. Place breast side down in a microwave-safe dish. Calculate the cooking time at 15 to 20 minutes per kilogram (7 to 9 minutes per pound). Cook for about 5 minutes at 100%, then

lower the power level to 70%. Turn the chicken onto its back halfway through the cooking time. When the cooking is finished, allow the bird to stand for 5 to 10 minutes before serving.

MICROTIPS

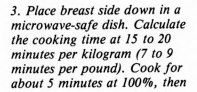

Cooking Bags

1. Never use a metal tie to close a cooking bag that is to go into the microwave oven. It could cause an arc and seriously damage your oven. Plastic ties that are perfectly safe for microwave use are available.

2. If you do not have plastic ties, cut a narrow strip off the bag and use it to tie the bag shut. If you plan to use cooking bags frequently, be sure to have a supply of ties on hand.

3. To be sure that the bag is not too securely fastened, wrap the neck of the bag around the handle of a wooden spoon. Then twist the tie around the bag and handle together, and remove the spoon.

Cooking Poultry

Type of Piece	Quantity	Cooking Time	Standing Time
Whole chicken		22 min/kg (10 min/lb) at 70%	10 min (covered with aluminum foil)
Quarters		22 min/kg (10 min/lb) at 70%	5 min
Wings	1 kg (2.2 lb) 450 g (1 lb)	15 to 18 min 8 min at 90%	5 min 5 min
Drumsticks	4 x 125 g (4 oz)	8 to 10 min at 70%	2 min
Whole turkey		29 min/kg (13 min/lb) at 70%	20 min (covered with aluminum foil)
Cornish game hen	2	20 to 22 min/kg (9 or 10 min/lb) at 70%	10 min
Duckling		26 min/kg (12 min/lb) at 70%	10 min (covered with aluminum foil)

Microwave cooking generally requires less fat (butter or oil) than conventional cooking. As a result, there are considerably fewer calories per portion.

MICROTIPS

To Cook a Chicken Successfully

Wash the chicken and dry it well before cooking. If you want the skin to be golden, either leave the chicken uncovered as it cooks or cover it with waxed paper. It is also possible to brown the chicken in the microwave using a special type of dish or it may be browned in a conventional oven after it is cooked. To ensure that the chicken cooks evenly, turn the dish around from time to time. Test for doneness by piercing the meat in the thigh. The bird is done when the juice released is clear and the thigh comes away easily.

How to Cook Poultry with Less Fat

As microwave cooking produces more fat than conventional cooking, it is not unusual for a large amount of fat to be released during cooking. You can simply pour it out of the dish before adding the accompanying sauce. Alternatively, you may use some of the cooking juices in the sauce itself. For the actual cooking, it is a good idea to set the chicken on an overturned plate in the cooking dish so that it does not sit in its own fat and juices.

Glazes and Sauces for Turkey

With paprika

125 mL (1/2 cup)
commercially available
chicken concentrate
50 mL (1/4 cup) melted
butter
paprika

Method

— Mix the concentrate and
the melted butter; brush
over the turkey.
— Sprinkle the bird with
paprika.

With soy sauce

10 mL (2 teaspoons)
cornstarch
50 mL (1/4 cup) soy sauce
150 mL (2/3 cup) cold water

Method

— Stir the cornstarch into
the cold water, blend well
and add the soy sauce.
— Cook at 100% until the
sauce thickens, stirring at
one-minute intervals.
— Brush over the turkey.

With tapioca

225 mL (7-3/4 oz) tapioca
pudding, available at your
supermarket
45 mL (3 tablespoons) corn
syrup
10 mL (2 teaspoons) lemon
juice
3 mL (1/2 teaspoon)
cinnamon
lemon zest to taste

Method

— Mix all the ingredients
together and brush over
the turkey.

Roast Turkey

Level of Difficulty	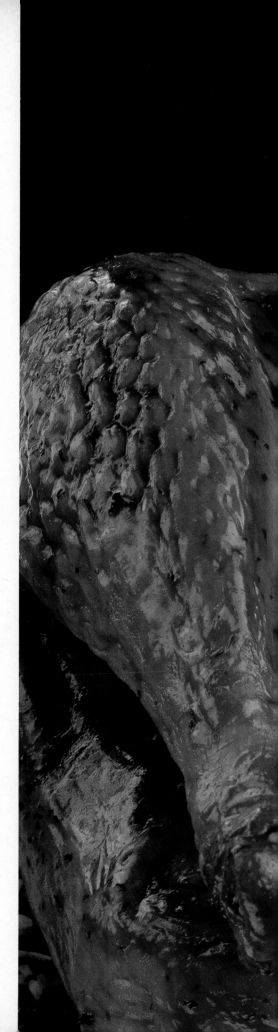 (utensils icon)
Preparation Time	10 min
Cost per Serving	$ $
Number of Servings	20 x 125 g (4 oz)
Nutritional Value	363 calories 34.7 g protein 2.9 mg iron
Food Exchanges	4 oz meat 1 fat exchange
Cooking Time	29 min/kg (13 min/lb)
Standing Time	20 min
Power Level	70%
Write Your Cooking Time Here	(pencil and apple icon)

Ingredients
1 turkey, 5 kg (11 lb)
125 mL (1/2 cup) chicken stock
50 mL (1/4 cup) melted butter

Method
— Mix the chicken stock and the butter together to make the glaze.
— Prepare the turkey and brush it with the glaze; season to taste.
— Put the turkey in a cooking bag and place in a microwave-safe dish.
— Cook at 70% for about 29 min/kg (13 min/lb), turning the turkey over once, two-thirds of the way through the cooking time. Allow to stand for 20 minutes before serving.

Braised Turkey with Vegetables

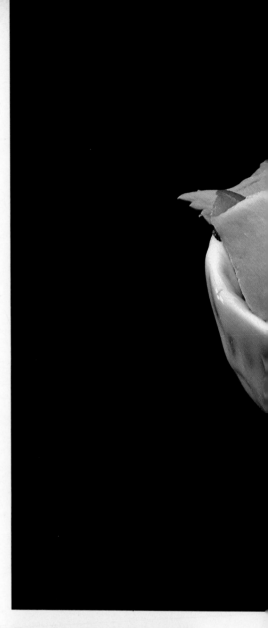

Level of Difficulty	🍴🍴
Preparation Time	30 min
Cost per Serving	$
Number of Servings	4
Nutritional Value	326 calories 24.2 g protein 4.6 mg iron
Food Exchanges	3-1/2 oz meat 1 vegetable exchange 1 fat exchange
Cooking Time	12 min
Standing Time	5 min
Power Level	70%
Write Your Cooking Time Here	

Ingredients
900 g (2 lb) turkey breast
1 large tomato, cut into chunks
1 large onion, sliced
1 large green pepper, cut into strips
85 mL (1/3 cup) hot chicken stock
2 mL (1/2 teaspoon) red wine vinegar

Method
— Bone the turkey breast and remove the skin; cut into 2 cm (1 inch) pieces.
— Place the vegetables in a shallow casserole, toss lightly and arrange the turkey pieces on top.
— Blend the liquid ingredients and pour over the turkey and the vegetables.
— Cook at 70% for 5 minutes. Give the dish a half-turn and continue cooking for 7 minutes or until the turkey is done.
— Cover and allow to stand for 5 minutes.

Assemble the ingredients required for the recipe: boneless turkey breast, the vegetables, chicken stock and wine vinegar.

26

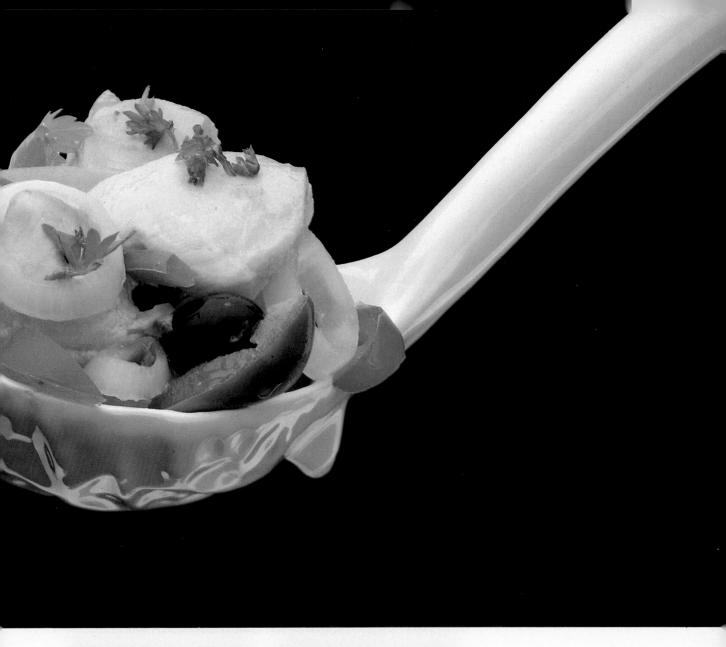

Place the vegetables in a microwave-safe dish and toss.

Arrange the pieces of turkey meat on top of the vegetables before you begin cooking the dish.

MICROTIPS

Reheating

Reheating food is one of the most practical uses of the microwave oven. It is important to know that the food being reheated should be stirred frequently so that the microwave energy is evenly distributed.

Turkey Escallops

Level of Difficulty	🍴
Preparation Time	20 min
Cost per Serving	$ $
Number of Servings	4
Nutritional Value	182 calories 26.5 g protein 2.1 mg iron
Food Exchanges	3 oz meat
Cooking Time	4 to 6 min
Standing Time	5 min
Power Level	70%
Write Your Cooking Time Here	

Ingredients
340 g (12 oz) turkey
escallops, 6 mm (1/4 inch)
thick
125 mL (1/2 cup) Corn
Flakes, crumbled
5 mL (1 teaspoon) dried
parsley
2 mL (1/2 teaspoon) lemon
pepper
10 mL (2 teaspoons) chopped
walnuts
1 egg yolk, beaten

Method
— Prepare the crumb coating
on a sheet of waxed paper
by combining the Corn
Flakes, dried parsley,
lemon pepper and
walnuts.
— Dip the escallops into the
beaten egg yolk and then
into the crumb coating.
— Arrange the escallops on a
platter and cook at 70%
for 2 minutes.
— Turn the escallops and
continue cooking at 70%
for 2 minutes or until they
are done. Allow to stand
for 5 minutes before
serving.
— If you wish, garnish with
asparagus.

*Assemble the required
ingredients. The escallops
should be 6 mm (1/4 inch)
thick.*

MICROTIPS

To Reduce a Recipe

To reduce a recipe by half, use half the quantity of each ingredient. To convert a recipe for 4 servings into 1 serving, the quantity of each ingredient is obviously divided by 4.

Be sure to use a cooking dish that is smaller in size to suit the amount required. It is important that the food reach a height in the oven the same as that in the original recipe.

If you have reduced a recipe by half, reduce the original cooking time by about a third. If you make a quarter recipe, cook it for approximately a third of the time. Check for doneness from time to time.

Keep to the same method and follow the same procedures as given in the original recipe.

Pay particular attention to details that affect the cooking, such as the starting temperature of the food being used. Foods with a high fat or sugar content will tend to cook very quickly.

Reduce the standing time by a few minutes from that specified in the original recipe.

Crumb Coatings

For chicken pieces with a crunchy, golden crust, nothing is better than a good crumb coating. Whether you choose to buy one of the commercial coatings or to make your own, the result is sure to please your guests. Also, your choice of coating enables you to vary the taste of a poultry dish without changing the method of cooking it. Another advantage in using a crumb coating is that it prevents lean parts from overcooking and becoming dried out.

A variety of ingredients, such as salted crackers, cereal, stale bread and graham crumbs, can be used in a crumb coating. You are limited only by your own preferences and your imagination. The flavor of a crumb coating can be enhanced by adding such ingredients as sesame seeds, poppyseeds and herbs. If the amount of fat in your diet is a concern, remove the skin, which contains the most fat, from the poultry piece before coating it with crumbs. For a quick and healthy meal or snack, serve breaded chicken pieces with raw or cooked broccoli or with a salad.

MICROTIPS

To Prepare a Turkey for Cooking

Traditionally, turkey has been defrosted by leaving it in the refrigerator for one or two days, depending on its size. This method requires planning ahead, something that many people no longer have time for. With a microwave oven, however, a whole turkey can be defrosted in just a few hours, although it must be watched to ensure that certain parts do not begin to cook before others are thawed. Also, a standing time of approximately an hour should be allowed before cooking.

The turkey must be completely defrosted before cooking.

Wash the turkey and wipe dry before cooking.

A space of at least 5 cm (2 inches) should be left between the turkey and the walls of the oven.

Glaze the turkey to enhance its appearance and to keep the meat tender.

Serve the turkey with stuffing.

Turkey Stew

Level of Difficulty	
Preparation Time	30 min
Cost per Serving	$ $
Number of Servings	4
Nutritional Value	375 calories 39.3 g protein 2.8 mg iron
Food Exchanges	4 oz meat 1/2 bread exchange 1 vegetable exchange 1 fat exchange
Cooking Time	40-45 min
Standing Time	10 min
Power Level	100%, 70%, 50%
Write Your Cooking Time Here	

Ingredients
450 g (1 lb) turkey breast, cubed
30 mL (2 tablespoons) butter
2 onions, cut into wedges
2 celery stalks, cut into sticks
2 carrots, cut into sticks
1 large green pepper, cut into cubes
2 potatoes, cubed
45 mL (3 tablespoons) flour
500 mL (2 cups) hot chicken stock
1 mL (1/4 teaspoon) marjoram
a few drops Tabasco sauce
salt and pepper

Method
— Melt the butter at 100% for 45 seconds; add the onions, celery and carrots and cook at 100% for 3 minutes.
— Add the cubes of turkey and cook at 70% for 7 minutes, or until they have lost their pink color.
— Add the flour and mix well; add seasoning to taste.
— Add the hot chicken stock, stir and add the green pepper and potatoes; bring to the boil by cooking at 100% for 8 minutes.
— Leave to simmer at 50% for 25 minutes.

Assemble the ingredients required for this recipe. The turkey breast should be cut into cubes.

MICROTIPS

To Cook Vegetables Evenly

Vegetables vary in shape and in density, and both these factors affect their cooking time. Therefore, cooking a variety of vegetables together can create a problem. To avoid this problem, cut the vegetables that cook slowly into smaller pieces, all the same size, and place them around the edge of the cooking dish. Put the vegetables that cook more quickly into the center of the dish. Any larger cuts should be placed away from the center so that the microwaves are more evenly distributed. Use the cooking time for those vegetables that cook the most quickly as your guide so as to avoid overcooking them. Turn halfway through the cooking time. When the time is up, check each vegetable for doneness and, if necessary, cook a little longer.

Rolled Turkey Roast with Herbs

Level of Difficulty	
Preparation Time	10 min
Cost per Serving	$ $
Number of Servings	5
Nutritional Value	380 calories 46.5 g protein 2.4 mg iron
Food Exchanges	5 oz meat 1 fat exchange
Cooking Time	19 min/kg (8 min/lb)
Standing Time	10 min
Power Level	70%
Write Your Cooking Time Here	

Ingredients
1 turkey roast, 675 g (1-1/2 lb), boned and rolled
1 or 2 cloves garlic
50 mL (1/4 cup) melted butter
5 mL (1 teaspoon) rosemary
5 mL (1 teaspoon) marjoram
15 mL (1 tablespoon) parsley
pepper

Method
— Stick the clove(s) of garlic into the turkey roast.
— Prepare the glaze by mixing the melted butter with the rosemary, marjoram, parsley and pepper.
— Place the roast in a cooking bag and pour in the glaze; close the bag, taking care to leave a small opening for the steam to escape, and place the bag and its contents in a shallow dish.
— Cook at 70% for 19 min/kg (8 min/lb), turning the turkey over halfway through the cooking time.
— Allow to stand for 10 minutes in the bag before serving.

The ingredients required for this recipe are a boned and rolled turkey roast, garlic, butter, spices and parsley.

Put the roast in a cooking bag and pour the glaze made with butter, spices and parsley into the bag over the turkey. Place in a shallow dish.

Spread the glaze evenly and close the bag, leaving a small opening for the steam to escape.

Halfway through the cooking time, turn the turkey over in its bag. Proceed with the cooking and allow to stand before serving.

Turkey and Bacon Croquettes

Level of Difficulty	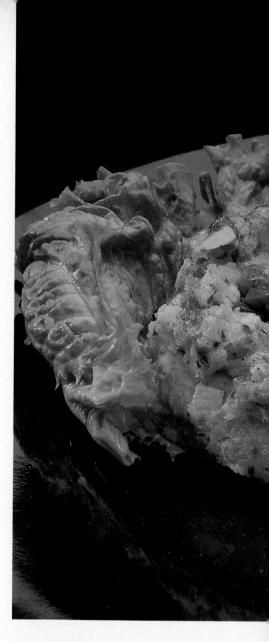
Preparation Time	40 min
Cost per Serving	$
Number of Servings	4
Nutritional Value	409 calories 40.7 g protein 2.8 mg iron
Food Exchanges	4 oz meat 1/2 bread exchange 1-1/2 fat exchanges
Cooking Time	15 min
Standing Time	2 min
Power Level	100%, 70%
Write Your Cooking Time Here	

Ingredients

Croquettes:
450 g (1 lb) cooked turkey, minced
2 eggs
45 mL (3 tablespoons) Italian breadcrumbs
45 mL (3 tablespoons) finely chopped onion
2 mL (1/2 teaspoon) salt
1 mL (1/4 teaspoon) sage
0.5 mL (1/8 teaspoon) pepper
paprika
4 slices bacon

Filling:
10 mL (2 teaspoons) butter
50 mL (1/4 cup) fresh mushrooms, chopped
50 mL (1/4 cup) zucchini, finely chopped
45 mL (3 tablespoons) Italian breadcrumbs
salt and pepper

Method

— Combine all the croquette ingredients, except the paprika and bacon, and divide evenly into 4.
— Shape into 4 croquettes, 2 cm (1 inch) thick and, pressing with your thumb, make a dent in the center of each. Set aside.
— To make the filling, melt the butter at 100% for 30 seconds, add the mushrooms and zucchini and cook at 100% for 3 to 4 minutes. Add the breadcrumbs and seasoning and mix well. Stuff the croquettes with this mixture.
— Cook the slices of bacon at 100% for 2-1/2 minutes.
— Cover each croquette with a slice of cooked bacon, folding the ends under the croquette.
— Place on a rack and cook at 70% for 4 minutes, give the rack a half-turn and continue cooking at 70% for another 4 minutes.
— Sprinkle with paprika and allow to stand for 2 minutes before serving.

Assemble all the ingredients required for the croquettes and the filling.

Make a dent in the center of each croquette and spoon the filling into it.

Place a slice of bacon over each croquette, folding the ends under the croquette.

Turkey Roulades with Spinach Filling

Level of Difficulty	🍴🍴
Preparation Time	30 min
Cost per Serving	$ $ $
Number of Servings	4
Nutritional Value	340 calories 42.8 g protein 4.2 mg iron
Food Exchanges	4 oz meat 1 vegetable exchange 1 fat exchange
Cooking Time	15 min
Standing Time	None
Power Level	70%
Write Your Cooking Time Here	

Ingredients

Turkey Roulades:
4 turkey escallops
15 mL (1 tablespoon) butter
30 mL (2 tablespoons) green onions, finely chopped
1 mL (1/4 teaspoon) garlic powder
1 mL (1/4 teaspoon) dried thyme
284 g (10 oz) package of frozen chopped spinach
125 mL (1/2 cup) Swiss cheese, grated

Crumb Coating:
125 mL (1/2 cup) Corn Flakes, crumbled
15 mL (1 tablespoon) parsley
5 mL (1 teaspoon) paprika
30 mL (2 tablespoons) butter, melted

Method

— Place the escallops between two sheets of waxed paper and pound them until they are only 3 mm (1/8 inch) thick.
— In a 500 mL (2 cup) casserole, combine the butter, green onions, garlic powder and thyme. Cover and cook at 70% for 1-1/2 to 2-1/2 minutes, or until the green onions are tender.
— Place the spinach in a shallow dish, cook at 70% for 4 to 5 minutes and drain. Add the cooked green onion mixture and the cheese and blend well.
— Place a quarter of this mixture on each escallop,

Pound each escallop between 2 sheets of waxed paper until it is just 3 mm (1/8 inch) thick.

Cook the spinach separately and drain it well, using a sieve.

Add the cooked green onion mixture and the cheese to the spinach. Mix well to obtain an even consistency.

Put a quarter of the mixture onto each escallop, spread evenly, roll up and secure with a toothpick.

Roll the stuffed escallops in melted butter and dip them in the crumb coating.

Arrange the stuffed and breaded escallops in a shallow dish, the opening secured with the toothpick facing downwards.

spread evenly, roll up and secure with a toothpick.
— Combine the dry ingredients for the crumb coating.
— Roll the stuffed escallops in the melted butter and coat them with the crumbs.

— Arrange the escallops on a rack in a dish, taking care to have the open side facing downwards.
— Cook at 70% for 4 minutes, give the dish a half-turn and continue cooking at 70% for another 4 minutes, or

until the escallops are done.

Tomatoes Stuffed with Turkey

Level of Difficulty	🍴🍴
Preparation Time	30 min
Cost per Serving	$
Number of Servings	8
Nutritional Value	381 calories 22.1 g protein 2.4 mg iron
Food Exchanges	2-1/2 oz meat 2 vegetable exchanges 3 fat exchanges
Cooking Time	3 min
Standing Time	None
Power Level	100%
Write Your Cooking Time Here	✏️

Ingredients
8 large tomatoes
450 g (1 lb) cooked turkey, diced
4 sticks celery, thinly sliced
45 mL (3 tablespoons) green onions, finely chopped
125 mL (1/2 cup) chopped walnuts
125 mL (1/2 cup) mayonnaise
30 mL (2 tablespoons) lemon juice
30 mL (2 tablespoons) parsley
30 mL (2 tablespoons) butter
15 mL (1 tablespoon) flour
2 mL (1/2 teaspoon) dry mustard
175 mL (3/4 cup) 18% cream
salt and pepper

Method
— Prepare each tomato using one of the methods described on page 42.

The first technique is the simpler of the two. We recommend it for anyone who feels intimidated by the more complex method.

Use a sharp knife to cut a thin slice from the top of each tomato.

Make 8 vertical cuts down the sides of the tomato, taking care not to cut through the base. Scoop the tomato pulp from the inside.

For a more decorative effect, choose the second method. It does, however, require more skill.

Using a sharp knife, cut around the top of the tomato in a zig-zag pattern.

Lift off the top and reserve for garnishing the finished dish. Scoop the tomato pulp from the inside.

— Put the prepared tomatoes in the refrigerator while you prepare the filling.
— Combine the turkey, celery, green onions, walnuts, mayonnaise, lemon juice and parsley and add the salt and pepper.

— Melt the butter, stir in the flour and mustard and add the cream.
— Cook at 100%. Stir the sauce at one-minute intervals and cook for 3 minutes or until it thickens.

— Add the sauce to the turkey mixture, stuff the tomatoes and serve.

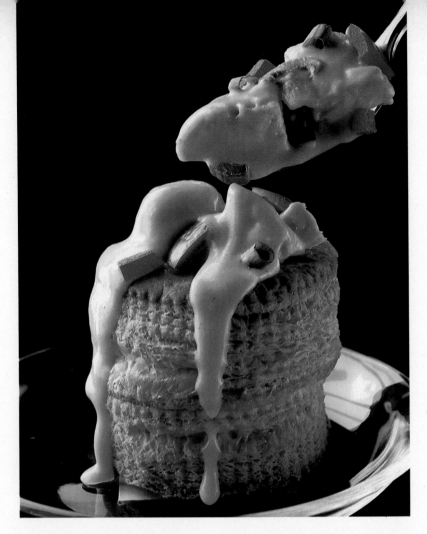

Turkey with Paprika

Ingredients
450 g (1 lb) cooked turkey, diced
3 green onions, sliced
1 green pepper, diced
1 red pepper, diced
125 g (4 oz) mushrooms, thinly sliced
60 mL (4 tablespoons) butter
30 mL (2 tablespoons) flour
15 mL (1 tablespoon) powdered chicken concentrate
50 mL (1/4 cup) milk
15 mL (1 tablespoon) paprika
8 vol-au-vent cases

Level of Difficulty	🍴
Preparation Time	15 min
Cost per Serving	$
Number of Servings	4
Nutritional Value	339 calories 40.3 g protein 1.8 mg iron
Food Exchanges	4 oz meat 1/4 milk exchange 1 fat exchange
Cooking Time	13 min
Standing Time	None
Power Level	100%, 70%
Write Your Cooking Time Here	

Method
— Mix the vegetables together and cook at 100% for 3 to 5 minutes; add the cooked turkey and set aside.
— Melt the butter at 100% for 40 seconds, add the flour and the chicken concentrate and add the milk.
— Stir well and cook at 100% for 4 to 5 minutes, stirring every 2 minutes.
— Add the paprika, stir into the turkey and vegetables and reheat at 70% for 3 minutes.
— Serve in hot vol-au-vent cases.

Roast Duck with Orange Sauce

Level of Difficulty	
Preparation Time	20 min
Cost per Serving	$ $ $
Number of Servings	4
Nutritional Value	478 calories 49.7 g protein 3.4 mg iron
Food Exchanges	5 oz meat 1/2 bread exchange 1/2 fruit exchange 1/2 fat exchange
Cooking Time	29 min/kg (12 min/lb)
Standing Time	10 min
Power Level	100%, 70%
Write Your Cooking Time Here	

Ingredients
1 duck, 2 kg (4-5 lb)
1 onion, cut into 8 wedges
salt and pepper

Sauce:
juice and zest of 1 large orange
10 mL (2 teaspoons) cornstarch
140 mL (5/8 cup) fresh orange juice
50 mL (1/4 cup) sherry
45 mL (3 tablespoons) wine vinegar
15 mL (1 tablespoon) extra fine granulated sugar
140 mL (5/8 cup) chicken or duck stock
salt and pepper

Method
— Peel the orange and cut the zest into thin strips. Cut the orange into two and squeeze out the juice.
— Stir the cornstarch into this juice, add the orange zest, the additional orange juice, the sherry, wine vinegar and sugar.
— Leave uncovered and heat at 100% for 3 to 4 minutes or until the sauce thickens, stirring twice.
— Add the stock and adjust the seasoning if necessary. Put to one side.
— Insert the onion wedges into the duck's cavity, prick the skin, and put the duck on a rack, breast side down.
— Cook at 70% for half the required time (29 min/kg or 12 min/lb), turn the dish and turn the duck over.
— Brush with the sauce and continue cooking. Allow to stand for 10 minutes. Serve with the orange sauce.

Before cooking, close up the duck, remembering to fasten the skin around the neck with a toothpick.

MICROTIPS

Defrosting Pieces of Duck

To defrost pieces of duck, use the following method: put them in the microwave oven and heat them at 30%, allowing 15 minutes for each 225 g (1/2 lb) of meat, with standing periods of equal length throughout the process. Allow to stand for 15 minutes before cooking.

Cooking Duck

As the skin of a duck is quite fatty it quickly turns a beautiful golden color, even in the microwave oven. As a result, putting it under the broiler in a conventional oven is unnecessary.

Prick the skin with a fork before cooking so that the fat can escape. Pierce the flesh of the thigh close to the breast and, if the juices run clear, the duck is done.

Quails with Green Grapes

Level of Difficulty	🍴🔪
Preparation Time	15 min
Cost per Serving	$ $ $
Number of Servings	4
Nutritional Value	252 calories 28.7 g protein 4.5 mg iron
Food Exchanges	3 oz meat 1 fat exchange
Cooking Time	10 min
Standing Time	3 min
Power Level	70%, 100%
Write Your Cooking Time Here	

Ingredients
8 quails
50 mL (1/4 cup) lemon juice

Sauce:
15 mL (1 tablespoon) butter
15 mL (1 tablespoon) flour
50 mL (1/4 cup) milk
45 mL (3 tablespoons) white wine
125 mL (1/2 cup) chicken stock
5 mL (1 teaspoon) lemon zest
125 mL (1/2 cup) green grapes

Method
— Brush the quails with the lemon juice, tie them and arrange them on a rack with the legs pointing into the center.
— Cook at 70% for 5 minutes or until the birds are done. Cover and allow to stand for 3 minutes.
— Prepare the sauce by melting the butter and adding the flour and stirring in the milk, wine, chicken stock and lemon zest. Cook at 100% until the sauce thickens. Add the grapes.
— Pour the sauce over the quails.

Assemble the ingredients required for this simple and delicious dish, which will impress your guests.

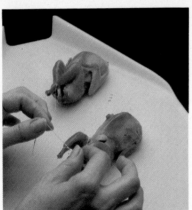

Use strong string to tie the quails so that they hold their shape during the cooking.

Mix the sauce ingredients together.

Arrange the quails on a rack for cooking, legs toward the center and breast side up.

Chicken Kiev

Level of Difficulty	🍴🍴
Preparation Time	45 min
Cost per Serving	$ $
Number of Servings	4
Nutritional Value	309 calories 31 g protein 5.6 mg iron
Food Exchanges	4 oz meat 2 fat exchanges
Cooking Time	8 min
Standing Time	None
Power Level	70%
Write Your Cooking Time Here	

Ingredients
2 whole chicken breasts,
boned and cut in half
2 egg yolks, beaten

Flavored Butter:
50 mL (1/4 cup) butter
1 mL (1/4 teaspoon) chives
pinch white pepper
2 cloves garlic, crushed

Crumb Coating:
125 mL (1/2 cup) Corn
Flakes, crumbled
60 mL (4 tablespoons)
Parmesan cheese, grated
5 mL (1 teaspoon) parsley,
chopped
5 mL (1 teaspoon) paprika

Method
— Blend the ingredients to
  make the flavored butter.
  Chill.
— Place the breasts between
  two sheets of waxed paper
  and pound them with a
  mallet until they are only
  6 mm (1/4 inch) thick.
— Mix the ingredients for the
  crumb coating. Set aside.
— Put a knob of flavored
  butter on each breast, roll
  up and secure with a
  toothpick. Dip each breast
  into the beaten egg yolks
  and then into the crumb
  coating.
— Arrange the breasts in a
  shallow casserole dish and
  cook uncovered at 70%
  for 4 minutes, turning the
  dish halfway through the
  cooking time.
— Move the breasts from the
  edge of the dish toward its
  center and continue
  cooking at 70% for
  another 4 minutes or until
  they are done.

Place the breasts between two sheets of waxed paper and pound them with a mallet until they are only 6 mm (1/4 inch) thick.

Put a knob of seasoned butter on each breast and carefully roll up.

Dip the rolled breasts into the beaten egg and then coat with the crumb mixture before cooking.

Chicken Stuffed with Celery and Nuts

Level of Difficulty	🍴
Preparation Time	20 min
Cost per Serving	$
Number of Servings	4
Nutritional Value	404 calories 36.0 g protein 2.8 mg iron
Food Exchanges	4-1/2 oz meat 1 vegetable exchange 1 fat exchange
Cooking Time	22 min/kg (10 min/lb)
Standing Time	10 min
Power Level	100%, 70%
Write Your Cooking Time Here	

Ingredients
1 chicken, 900 g (2 lb)
15 mL (1 tablespoon) butter
15 mL (1 tablespoon) powdered chicken concentrate

Stuffing:
1 stick celery, thinly sliced
1 onion, finely diced
45 mL (3 tablespoons) butter
45 mL (3 tablespoons) chopped nuts
100 mL (3/8 cup) ready-made breadcrumbs
juice and grated zest of 1/2 orange

Method
— Melt the butter at 100% for 20 seconds, add the chicken concentrate and set aside.

— To prepare the stuffing, cook the celery and onion at 100% for 2 minutes, add the remaining ingredients and season to taste.
— Stuff the chicken and brush it with the mixture of butter and chicken concentrate.
— Put the chicken on a rack and cook at 70% for 22 min/kg (10 min/lb), turning halfway through the cooking time.
— Allow to stand for 10 minutes before serving.

Saffron Chicken

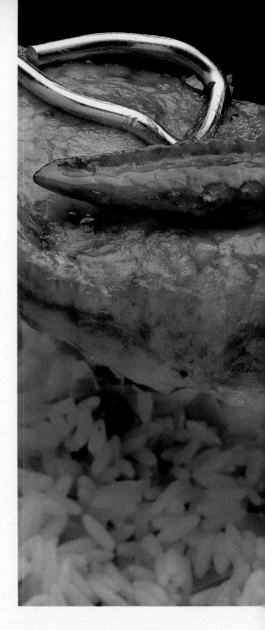

Level of Difficulty	🍴
Preparation Time	15 min
Cost per Serving	$
Number of Servings	4
Nutritional Value	360 calories 27.1 g protein 2.8 mg iron
Food Exchanges	4 oz meat 1 milk exchange 1 vegetable exchange 1 fat exchange
Cooking Time	22 min/kg (10 min/lb) plus 16 min
Standing Time	5 min
Power Level	100%, 70%
Write Your Cooking Time Here	

Ingredients
1 chicken, 1 to 1.5 kg (2 to 3 lb), cut into serving pieces
125 mL (1/2 cup) celery, finely chopped
125 mL (1/2 cup) onion, finely chopped
300 mL (1-1/4 cups) hot chicken stock
15 mL (1 tablespoon) parsley
pepper
5 mL (1 teaspoon) saffron
250 mL (1 cup) rice
30 mL (2 tablespoons) melted butter
30 mL (2 tablespoons) powdered chicken concentrate
1 284 mL (10 oz) can cream of mushroom soup

Method
— Cook the celery and onion at 100% for 4 minutes and add the hot chicken stock, seasoning and rice.
— Cover and cook at 100% for 5 minutes, reduce the power level to 70% and continue cooking for 7 minutes.
— Brush the chicken with a mixture of the melted butter and the chicken concentrate.
— Spread the rice mixture over the bottom of a casserole dish, add the cream of mushroom soup and place the chicken on top, arranging the pieces so the thicker parts face the outside of the dish.
— Cover and cook at 70% for 22 min/kg (10 min/lb), turning the dish halfway through the cooking time.
— Leave the cover on and allow to stand for 5 minutes before serving.

First cook the celery and onion, then add the chicken stock, seasoning and the rice and cook in a shallow dish.

When the rice has absorbed the stock, add the cream of mushroom soup and the chicken pieces. Arrange the chicken so that the thicker parts face the outside of the dish.

Cover with plastic wrap. Turn the dish halfway through the cooking time to ensure even cooking.

Spices, Aromatics and Condiments for Poultry

The succulent meat of poultry is the perfect foil for virtually any flavor you may wish to add. Whether you choose marinating, seasoning or stewing in a subtly flavored stock, poultry takes on added flavor without losing its own distinctive taste—a taste that no cook would want to disguise. An additional advantage of poultry is that it can be prepared to suit a wide range of preferences. It can be lightly rubbed with seasoning for a subtle flavor or steeped in a marinade for a richer, heartier creation. Nature has provided us with a variety of seasonings to complement and enhance the delicious flavors of poultry.

Spices for Poultry and for Complementary Sauces

Spice	Fowl	Sauce
Basil	Duck	Orange
Bayleaves	Chicken fricassée	Marinades
Ginger	Stuffing	Marinades
Marjoram	Chicken with cream Stuffing Goose	Sour cream
Nutmeg	Chicken	Cream
Curry powder	Chicken	Marinades
Rosemary	Partridge Capon Duck	Barbecue
Savory	Chicken Stuffing	Horseradish
Sage	Goose Turkey Stuffing	

For Marinades

Marinades	
Main Ingredient	**Comments**
Soy sauce	Imparts a lovely golden color and a tangy flavor.
Tarragon vinegar	The acid softens the meat fibers so they take on the flavor of the herbs and spices.
Red wine vinegar	Softens the meat so it takes on the flavor of other seasonings.
Red wine	Adds a full, rich flavor. Add cayenne and onions to enhance the flavor of the marinade.
Olive oil	Rub over the surface of the bird and leave to marinate for several hours before cooking. Imparts a beautiful golden color.

There is no end to the variety of seasonings you can use in marinades. Let your imagination go and feel free to experiment.

You can choose any of the following herbs.

Tarragon. This herb has a sharp taste, faintly reminiscent of aniseed when it is fresh. It is best used alone and with a certain amount of restraint. It can also be used in stuffing.

Parsley. The curly varieties have more flavor. Parsley goes well with all herbs.

Basil. Best used alone. Its sweetness makes it the ideal herb to counteract the acid in tomato marinades.

Sage. The rather strong flavor of this herb requires that it be used with discretion. It is traditionally used in stuffings.

Rosemary. Strong and spicy. Use in moderation.

Oregano. Dried oregano adds a strong flavor. Enhances marinades and tomato sauces.

You can choose from an equally wide range of spices. The following list is far from exhaustive.

Nutmeg. Enhances the flavor of marinades and goes well in cream sauces. Use sparingly.

Cloves. The pronounced flavor of cloves goes well in full-bodied marinades for barbecue cooking.

Cinnamon. The sweet flavor of this spice is suitable for use in stuffing to accompany duck.

Paprika. Used for both its flavor and its color.

Saffron, cumin, coriander, mace and **juniper berries.** Each, having its own distinctive flavor, can be used to make your food even more delicious.

Chicken Salad

Ingredients
375 mL (1-1/2 cups) cooked chicken, cut into strips
30 mL (2 tablespoons) butter
75 mL (1/3 cup) almonds
175 mL (3/4 cup) plain yogurt
15 mL (1 tablespoon) Dijon mustard
75 mL (1/3 cup) bamboo shoots
125 mL (1/2 cup) red pepper, cut into strips
125 mL (1/2 cup) green pepper, cut into strips
75 mL (1/3 cup) celery, cut into strips
15 mL (1 tablespoon) parsley
lettuce leaves

Level of Difficulty	🍴
Preparation Time	15 min
Cost per Serving	$ $
Number of Servings	4
Nutritional Value	201 calories 23.8 g protein 1.3 mg iron
Food Exchanges	2-1/2 oz meat 1 vegetable exchange
Cooking Time	5 min
Standing Time	None
Power Level	100%
Write Your Cooking Time Here	

Method
— Melt the butter at 100% for 1 minute, add the almonds and roast them at 100% for 3 to 4 minutes or until they are sufficiently browned, stirring every minute.
— Pour off the butter and dry the roasted almonds.
— Prepare the sauce by combining the yogurt and the Dijon mustard.
— Add the almonds and all the other ingredients except the lettuce and mix into the sauce.
— Serve the salad on lettuce leaves.

All-Purpose Chicken Base

Level of Difficulty	⬛
Preparation Time	30 min
Cost per Serving	$
Number of Servings	4 x 4
Nutritional Value	472 calories 70.3 g protein 4.6 mg iron
Cooking Time	30 to 35 min
Standing Time	None
Power Level	90%
Write Your Cooking Time Here	

Ingredients
assorted chicken pieces, 3.5 to 4 kg (8 to 9 lb)
50 mL (1/4 cup) flour
1 onion, diced
1 carrot, diced
30 mL (2 tablespoons) powdered chicken concentrate
15 mL (1 tablespoon) dried parsley
5 mL (1 teaspoon) salt
2 mL (1/2 teaspoon) basil
2 mL (1/2 teaspoon) marjoram
1 mL (1/4 teaspoon) pepper

Method
— Arrange the chicken in a shallow dish and sprinkle with flour.
— Add the remaining ingredients, cover and cook at 90% for 30 to 35 minutes, or until the meat loses its pink color, stirring several times during the cooking.
— Remove the chicken from the cooking juices, remove the bones and cut the meat into bite-sized cubes.
— Put the chicken cubes back into the liquid, allow to cool completely and freeze in 4 equal portions.

Some of the recipes in this book call for cooked chicken. We have therefore devised this basic recipe for cooking chicken, which can be frozen and then thawed when needed. It can be diced, minced, or served in any number of other ways. By having the chicken cooked ahead, you can have a delicious meal ready in no time.

Chicken with Rice Pilaf

Ingredients
1/4 basic cooked chicken recipe, defrosted (see recipe on page 58)
125 mL (1/2 cup) celery, diced
125 mL (1/2 cup) green pepper, diced
10 mL (2 teaspoons) olive oil
250 mL (1 cup) long grain rice
500 mL (2 cups) hot chicken stock
5 mL (1 teaspoon) chives
1 mL (1/4 teaspoon) salt
1 bayleaf
125 mL (1/2 cup) cashew nuts

Level of Difficulty	🍴
Preparation Time	10 min
Cost per Serving	$ $
Number of Servings	4
Nutritional Value	340 calories 22.8 g protein 2.7 mg iron
Food Exchanges	3 oz meat 1 bread exchange 1 vegetable exchange
Cooking Time	16 min
Standing Time	3 min
Power Level	100%, 70%
Write Your Cooking Time Here	

Method
— Combine the celery, green pepper and oil; cover and cook at 100% for 2 to 3 minutes, or until the vegetables are tender.
— Add the rice, hot chicken stock, seasoning and chicken.
— Cover and cook at 100% for 5 minutes, reduce the power level to 70% and continue to cook for 8 minutes.
— Add the cashew nuts, cover again and allow to stand for 3 minutes before serving.

Chicken with Dumplings

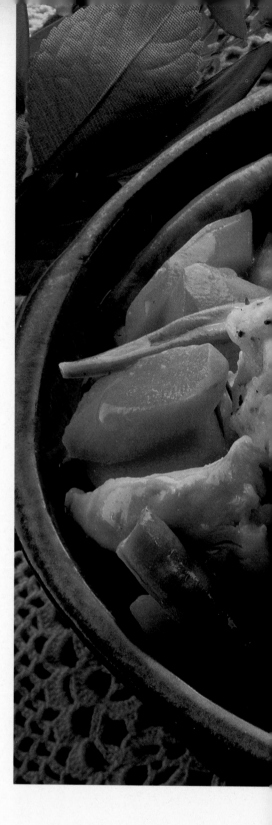

Level of Difficulty	
Preparation Time	15 min
Cost per Serving	$
Number of Servings	4
Nutritional Value	472 calories 29 g protein 3.6 mg iron
Food Exchanges	3 oz meat 2 vegetable exchanges 2 bread exchanges 1 fat exchange
Cooking Time	25 min
Standing Time	None
Power Level	100%
Write Your Cooking Time Here	

Ingredients

Chicken:
1/4 basic cooked chicken
recipe, defrosted (see recipe
on page 58)
45 mL (3 tablespoons) flour
375 mL (1-1/2 cups) carrots,
sliced
875 mL (3-1/2 cups) potato,
diced
375 mL (1-1/2 cups) chicken
stock
2 mL (1/2 teaspoon) salt
0.5 mL (1/8 teaspoon)
rosemary
0.5 mL (1/8 teaspoon)
pepper

Dumpling Batter:
375 mL (1-1/2 cups) flour
15 mL (1 tablespoon) dried
parsley
1 mL (1/4 teaspoon) savory
10 mL (2 teaspoons) baking
powder
2 mL (1/2 teaspoon) salt
1 egg
150 mL (2/3 cup) milk
30 mL (2 tablespoons) salad
oil
30 mL (2 tablespoons)
poppyseeds

Method
— Put the chicken into a casserole dish, add the flour and mix. Add all the other ingredients for the chicken, cover and cook at 100% for 20 minutes, stirring halfway through the cooking time.

— Mix all the dry ingredients for the dumpling batter together. In a separate bowl, beat the egg, milk and oil. Combine the two mixtures and beat to an even consistency.
— Drop the batter by spoonfuls over the chicken

around the edge of the pan.
— Cover and cook at 100% for 5 minutes, or until the batter is properly cooked.

Chicken with Wine and Herbs

Level of Difficulty	🍴
Preparation Time	10 min
Cost per Serving	$ $
Number of Servings	4
Nutritional Value	377 calories 57 g protein 2.9 mg iron
Food Exchanges	5 oz meat 1 bread exchange
Cooking Time	60 min
Standing Time	None
Power Level	100%, 90%, 70%
Write Your Cooking Time Here	

Ingredients
1 chicken, 1.3 kg (3 lb)
1 onion, quartered
2 cloves garlic
1 284 mL (10 oz) can beef consommé
125 mL (1/2 cup) white wine
125 mL (1/2 cup) water
5 mL (1 teaspoon) rosemary
5 mL (1 teaspoon) marjoram
salt and pepper
125 mL (1/2 cup) long grain rice

Method
— Put 1 onion quarter and 1 clove garlic inside the chicken.
— Rub the skin of the chicken with the other clove of garlic and put the chicken in a casserole dish breast side down.
— Arrange the other 3 onion quarters around the chicken. Set aside.
— Mix the consommé with the wine and water, add the seasoning and bring to the boil at 100%.
— Pour the liquid over the chicken, cover the casserole and cook at 90% for 30 minutes.
— Turn the chicken over and baste. Give the dish a half-turn and add the rice.
— Cover the casserole again and continue cooking at 70% for 20 minutes, or until the chicken is done.

Assemble the ingredients required for this simple and tasty recipe.

MICROTIPS

To Avoid Soft, Moist Skin When Cooking Poultry

There is no doubt that poultry is a great favorite with owners of microwave ovens. Some cooks do complain, however, that the skin of poultry cooked in the microwave always remains soft and moist. There are several ways to remedy this situation.

One simple way of obtaining a crisper skin is to add a coating of bread or cracker crumbs. Alternatively the bird may be placed under the broiler of a conventional oven for a few minutes after microwaving is complete.

Another solution - and one which has the added virtue of significantly reducing the number of calories - is to remove the skin before cooking and brush the surface of the meat with a browning agent.

Lemon Chicken

Level of Difficulty	
Preparation Time	10 min
Cost per Serving	$
Number of Servings	6
Nutritional Value	187 calories 35.7 g protein 1.5 mg iron
Food Exchanges	3 oz meat 1 fat exchange
Cooking Time	22 min/kg (10 min/lb)
Standing Time	10 min
Power Level	70%, 100%
Write Your Cooking Time Here	

Ingredients
1 chicken, 2 kg (4.4 lb)
1 lemon
15 mL (1 tablespoon) parsley
paprika
10% cream
15 mL (1 tablespoon)
cornstarch
45 mL (3 tablespoons) cold
water

Method
— Grate the lemon zest and
  squeeze out the lemon
  juice.
— Brush the chicken with the
  lemon juice and sprinkle
  with parsley and paprika.
— Put the chicken on a rack
  and cook at 70% for 22
  min/kg (10 min/lb),
  turning the dish halfway
  through the cooking time.

— When the chicken is
  cooked cover with
  aluminum foil, keeping
  the shiny side in, and let
  stand for 10 minutes.
— Prepare the sauce by
  adding the cream to the
  cooking juices, to make
  up a total 500 mL (2 cups)
  liquid.
— Cook at 100%, stirring
  every 2 minutes.
— Thicken the mixture by
  adding the cornstarch,
  mixed with the water, and
  continue to cook at 100%
  for 2 minutes, stirring
  after 1 minute, and add
  the lemon rind.

*Select a dish to accommodate
the size of the chicken and place
a rack inside.*

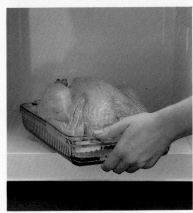

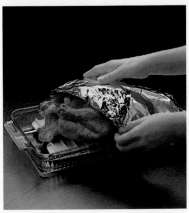

*Place the chicken on the rack
and squeeze or brush the lemon
juice over it. Sprinkle with
parsley and paprika.*

*Put the chicken in the oven.
Give the dish a half-turn
halfway through the cooking
time.*

*Wrap the cooked chicken in
aluminum foil, shiny side in,
while you prepare the sauce.*

Chicken with Orange

Level of Difficulty	
Preparation Time	15 min
Cost per Serving	$ $
Number of Servings	3
Nutritional Value	676 calories 35.6 g protein 3.1 mg iron
Food Exchanges	4 oz meat 1 fruit exchange 1-1/2 bread exchange
Cooking Time	23 min
Standing Time	10 min
Power Level	100%, 70%
Write Your Cooking Time Here	

Ingredients
6 chicken drumsticks
50 mL (1/4 cup) flour
5 mL (1 teaspoon) paprika
5 mL (1 teaspoon) salt
2 mL (1/2 teaspoon) pepper
50 mL (1/4 cup) oil
5 mL (1 teaspoon) orange zest
175 mL (3/4 cup) orange juice
125 mL (1/2 cup) marmalade
45 mL (3 tablespoons) cornstarch
125 mL (1/2 cup) cold water
50 mL (1/4 cup) almonds, sliced

Method
— Mix the paprika, salt and pepper with the flour and coat the chicken drumsticks.
— Preheat a browning dish at 100% for 7 minutes, add the oil and brown the chicken. Set aside.
— Combine the orange zest, juice and marmalade and heat at 100% for 1 to 2 minutes.
— Add the cornstarch to the cold water, make a smooth paste and stir into the sauce.
— Cook at 100% until the mixture thickens, stirring at one-minute intervals.
— Arrange the drumsticks so that the thicker parts are facing the outside of the dish, pour the sauce over them and add the almonds.
— Cover and cook at 70% for 18 to 20 minutes, stirring the mixture and giving the dish a half-turn halfway through the cooking time.
— Let stand for 10 minutes before serving.

Coat the chicken well by shaking it in a bag with the mixture of flour, paprika, salt and pepper.

Preheat a browning dish so that you can sear the chicken drumsticks.

Arrange the drumsticks so that the thicker parts are facing the outside, pour the sauce over them, add the almonds and cover before putting into the oven.

Chicken Livers with Noodles

Level of Difficulty	
Preparation Time	15 min
Cost per Serving	$
Number of Servings	4
Nutritional Value	362 calories 31.6 g protein 9.97 mg iron
Food Exchanges	3 oz meat 1 bread exchange 1 vegetable exchange 1 fat exchange
Cooking Time	10 min*
Standing Time	None
Power Level	100%, 70%
Write Your Cooking Time Here	

* You must also include the time required to cook the noodles.

Ingredients

450 g (1 lb) chicken livers
225 g (1/2 lb) fettuccine
15 mL (1 tablespoon) butter
50 mL (1/4 cup) Parmesan cheese, grated
1 onion, thinly sliced
150 mL (2/3 cup) fresh mushrooms, thinly sliced
50 mL (1/4 cup) green pepper, finely chopped
1 tomato, thinly sliced
45 mL (3 tablespoons) fresh parsley, chopped
1 mL (1/4 teaspoon) salt
pinch garlic powder

Method

— Cook the fettuccine in the usual way, place in a casserole dish and add 5 mL (1 teaspoon) butter and the Parmesan cheese. Toss until the butter is melted and set aside.
— Put 10 mL (2 teaspoons) butter in another dish, add all the vegetables except the tomato and cook at 100% for 1-1/2 to 2 minutes, or until they soften. Add the tomato slices.
— Season and stir. Prick the chicken livers, add them and cook at 70% for 5 to 7 minutes, stirring halfway through the cooking time. Set aside.
— Heat the fettuccine at 100% for 1 minute and stir.
— Add the chicken livers and cooked vegetables.
— Sprinkle with grated Parmesan cheese before serving.

Prick the chicken livers with a fork before cooking them.

Cook the vegetables in the butter and then add the tomato slices.

Add the chicken livers to the vegetables, cook, reheat the fettuccine and cover with chicken liver and vegetable mixture.

Chicken Kebabs

Level of Difficulty	🍴
Preparation Time	10 min
Cost per Serving	$ $
Number of Servings	4
Nutritional Value	143 calories 20.5 g protein 1.5 mg iron
Food Exchanges*	2 oz meat 1 vegetable exchange
Cooking Time	8 min
Standing Time	None
Power Level	90%
Write Your Cooking Time Here	

* Based on ingredients specified.

Ingredients

Kebabs:
1 whole chicken breast, boned, skinned and diced
1 large green pepper, cut into large pieces
1 onion, quartered
12 whole mushrooms
other vegetables of your choice
1/2 orange with peel, cut into segments

Teriyaki Sauce:
15 mL (1 tablespoon) oil
15 mL (1 tablespoon) soy sauce
1 clove garlic, thinly sliced
5 mL (1 teaspoon) ground ginger
2 mL (1/2 teaspoon) sugar

Method
— Combine the ingredients for the sauce.
— Thread the ingredients onto wooden skewers, alternating the chicken cubes with the vegetables and the orange segments.
— Brush each kebab with the sauce.
— Arrange the kebabs on a platter and cook at 90% for 6 to 8 minutes, turning them halfway through the cooking time.

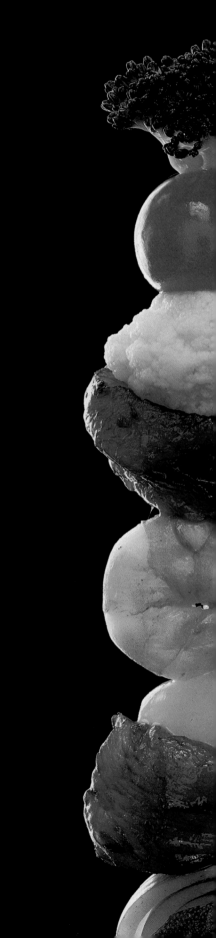

Chicken Wings with Garlic

Level of Difficulty	🍴
Preparation Time	5 min
Cost per Serving	$
Number of Servings	4
Nutritional Value	266 calories 27.2 g protein 2.1 mg iron
Food Exchanges	3 oz meat 1 sugar exchange
Cooking Time	20-25 min
Standing Time	5 min
Power Level	100%
Write Your Cooking Time Here	

Ingredients
1 kg (2.2 lb) chicken wings
1 341 mL (12 oz) jar VH sauce, available at your supermarket
50 mL (1/4 cup) brown sugar
2 cloves garlic, thinly sliced
30 mL (2 tablespoons) cornstarch
75 mL (1/3 cup) cold water

Method
— Combine the VH sauce, brown sugar and garlic and cook at 100% for 5 minutes, or until it comes to a boil.
— Mix the cornstarch with the water and add to the sauce.
— Arrange the chicken wings in a shallow dish and cover with the sauce.
— Cover and cook at 100% for 15 to 18 minutes, stirring halfway through the cooking time.
— Allow to stand for 5 minutes before serving.

Oriental Turkey

Ingredients
450 g (1 lb) turkey escallops, cut into strips
30 mL (2 tablespoons) oil
125 mL (1/2 cup) carrots, cut into sticks
125 mL (1/2 cup) broccoli florets
125 mL (1/2 cup) cauliflower florets
125 mL (1/2 cup) snow peas
2 green onions, cut lengthwise
2 cloves garlic, thinly sliced
5 mL (1 teaspoon) fresh or preserved ginger, chopped
250 mL (1 cup) hot chicken stock
15 mL (1 tablespoon) soy sauce
15 mL (1 tablespoon) cornstarch
50 mL (1/4 cup) cold water

Level of Difficulty	🍴🍴
Preparation Time	30 min
Cost per Serving	$ $
Number of Servings	4
Nutritional Value	330 calories 38.2 g protein 1.8 mg iron
Food Exchanges	3-1/2 oz meat 2 vegetable exchanges 1 fat exchange
Cooking Time	20 min
Standing Time	None
Power Level	100%, 70%
Write Your Cooking Time Here	

Method
— Preheat a browning dish at 100% for 7 minutes, add the oil and put back in the oven. Heat at 100% for 30 seconds.
— Brown the vegetables, garlic and ginger in the preheated dish and then add the turkey.
— Cook at 70% for 5 minutes.
— Add the chicken stock and the soy sauce and heat at 100% to boiling point.
— Add the cornstarch mixed with the cold water and cook 1 to 2 minutes at 100% until the sauce thickens.
— Serve as soon as it comes out of the oven.

Chicken Breasts Supreme

Level of Difficulty	🍴
Preparation Time	20 min
Cost per Serving	$ $
Number of Servings	4
Nutritional Value	468 calories 43.6 g protein 3.2 mg iron
Food Exchanges	5 oz meat 2 vegetable exchanges 1 fat exchange
Cooking Time	25-30 min
Standing Time	5 min
Power Level	100%, 70%
Write Your Cooking Time Here	

Ingredients
2 whole chicken breasts, boned, skinned and cut in half
90 mL (6 tablespoons) butter or oil
300 g (10 oz) mushrooms, sliced
90 mL (6 tablespoons) flour
1 L (4 cups) hot chicken stock
60 mL (4 tablespoons) tomato paste
lemon juice
90 mL (6 tablespoons) grated cheddar cheese
salt and pepper
noodles

Method
— Melt the butter at 100% for 2 minutes, add the chicken breasts and cook at 70% for 5 minutes. Or, preheat a browning dish at 100% for 7 minutes, add the oil and heat at 100% for 30 seconds, brown the chicken pieces then cook at 70% for 5 minutes.
— Remove the chicken from the dish, add the mushrooms to the remaining butter or oil and cook at 100% for 4 minutes.
— Add the flour and stir briskly to mix.
— Add the hot chicken stock and the tomato paste and stir.
— Add the chicken breasts to the sauce, cover and cook at 70% for 10 minutes.
— Add a few drops of lemon juice, the cheddar cheese, salt and pepper.
— Cook covered at 70% for 3 minutes and let stand for 5 minutes before serving.
— Cut the meat into bite-size pieces and serve on a bed of noddles.

Cook the chicken pieces or
brown them in a preheated
browning dish. Remove and set
aside.

Cook the mushrooms, add the
flour, chicken stock and tomato
paste. Add the chicken to the
sauce.

Add the lemon juice, grated
cheddar cheese and seasoning
before the final cooking.

Chicken Casserole

Level of Difficulty	🍴
Preparation Time	15 min
Cost per Serving	$
Number of Servings	4
Nutritional Value	483 calories 42.4 g protein 3.7 mg iron
Food Exchanges	4 oz meat 1 bread exchange 2 vegetable exchanges 1 fat exchange
Cooking Time	25 min
Standing Time	5 min
Power Level	100%, 70%
Write Your Cooking Time Here	

Ingredients
2 whole chicken breasts, cut in half
1 package onion soup
50 mL (1/4 cup) brown sugar
50 mL (1/4 cup) chili sauce
1 284 mL (10 oz) can cream of mushroom soup
150 mL (2/3 cup) water
4 potatoes, diced
4 carrots, sliced
1 onion, sliced
3 sticks celery, sliced

Method
— Combine all the ingredients.
— Cover and cook at 100% for 10 minutes, reduce the power level to 70% and continue to cook for 15 minutes or until the chicken breasts are done, stirring halfway through the cooking time.
— Leave cover on and let stand for 5 minutes.

Lemon Chicken
with Parsley

Level of Difficulty	
Preparation Time	30 min
Cost per Serving	$
Number of Servings	6
Nutritional Value	204 calories 25.6 g protein 2 mg iron
Food Exchanges	3 oz meat
Cooking Time	22 min/kg (10 min/lb)
Standing Time	None
Power Level	100%, 70%
Write Your Cooking Time Here	

Ingredients
1 chicken, 1.4 kg (3 lbs)
juice and zest of 1 lemon
30 mL (2 tablespoons)
chopped parsley
10 mL (2 teaspoons) tarragon
1 clove garlic, crushed
4 thin slices lemon, diced, for
garnish

Sauce:
juice of 1 lemon
10 mL (2 teaspoons) parsley
pinch basil
15 mL (1 tablespoon) butter
salt
15 mL (1 tablespoon)
cornstarch
water, approximately 125 mL
(1/2 cup)

Method
— Grate the zest of one
lemon and squeeze out the
juice. Add the parsley,
tarragon and garlic, and
heat at 100% for 40
seconds.
— Brush the chicken with
this mixture, arrange it on
a rack and cook at 70%
for 22 min/kg (10
min/lb).
— Remove the chicken and
wrap in aluminum foil,
shiny side in. Reserve the
cooking juices.
— Prepare the sauce by
mixing the lemon juice
with the cooking juices
and adding enough water
to make up 175 mL (3/4
cup) liquid.

— Add the seasoning,
thicken with cornstarch
dissolved in a little cold
water and cook at 70%
for 4 minutes, stirring
halfway through the
cooking time.
— When the sauce has
thickened, stir in the
butter.
— Unwrap the chicken, cut
into pieces and cover with
sauce. Garnish with diced
lemon and serve.

To enhance the flavor of a bird, rub the entire surface with a garlic clove.

It is also possible to create a liquid seasoning. Add herbs and other aromatics to a little lemon juice and brush the surface of the bird.

MICROTIPS

For Crisp Skin

If you do not want the skin to be too moist, cover the chicken with crumbled crackers or breadcrumbs before cooking. For really crisp skin, put the chicken under the broiler in a conventional oven after you have cooked it in the microwave.

Chicken with Ginger

Level of Difficulty	🍴
Preparation Time	15 min*
Cost per Serving	$
Number of Servings	6
Nutritional Value	262 calories 39.1 g protein 2.5 mg iron
Food Exchanges	4 oz meat 1/4 bread exchange
Cooking Time	23 min
Standing Time	3 min
Power Level	100%, 90%
Write Your Cooking Time Here	

* The chicken should be left to marinate for at least 6 hours.

Ingredients
1 chicken, 2 kg (4.4 lb), cut into serving pieces

Marinade:
125 mL (1/2 cup) chicken stock
85 mL (1/3 cup) soy sauce
30 mL (2 tablespoons) onion, finely chopped
1 clove garlic, crushed
15 mL (1 tablespoon) lime juice
15 mL (1 tablespoon) lime zest
7 mL (1-1/2 teaspoons) sesame oil

Crumb Coating:
10 wholewheat biscuits, crumbled
2 mL (1/2 teaspoon) garlic powder

5 mL (1 teaspoon) powdered ginger
1 egg yolk, beaten
5 mL (1 tablespoon) water

Method
— Combine the marinade ingredients and cook at 100% for 3 minutes, stirring halfway through the cooking time. Let the marinade cool.
— Lay the chicken pieces in the liquid and marinate in the refrigerator for 6 hours, turning them from time to time.
— Combine the dry ingredients for the crumb coating.
— Dry the chicken pieces.
— Beat the egg yolk with the water, dip the chicken pieces into the mixture and then into the crumb coating.
— Arrange the pieces of chicken on a rack so that the thickest parts face the outside of the dish and cook at 90% for 8 minutes.
— Turn the pieces around, give the rack a half-turn and continue to cook at 90% for 10 to 12 minutes or until the chicken is tender.
— Allow to stand for 3 minutes before serving.

Blend and cook the ingredients for the marinade, cool, add the chicken pieces and marinate in the refrigerator for 6 hours.

Remove the chicken pieces and dry them carefully with paper towel.

Dip the pieces into the egg yolk and the crumb coating and arrange them on a rack for cooking.

Chicken Hotpot

Level of Difficulty	🍴🍴
Preparation Time	40 min
Cost per Serving	$ $
Number of Servings	8
Nutritional Value	470 calories 38 g protein 3.7 mg iron
Food Exchanges	5 oz meat 1/4 bread exchange 2 vegetable exchanges
Cooking Time	50 min
Standing Time	10 min
Power Level	100%, 70%
Write Your Cooking Time Here	

Ingredients
1 chicken, 2 kg (4.4 lb)
625 mL (2-1/2 cups) water
8 carrots, sliced diagonally across
1 turnip, cut into sticks
8 leeks, sliced
2 stalks celery, cut into strips
8 cabbage leaves, parboiled
1 onion, studded with 5 cloves
1 bouquet garni
pinch allspice
salt and pepper

Stuffing:
450 g (1 lb) sausage meat
2 onions, finely chopped
2 cloves garlic, finely chopped
250 mL (1 cup) bread cubes soaked in milk (crusts removed)
30 mL (2 tablespoons) parsley, chopped
2 eggs

Method
— Combine ingredients for the stuffing.
— Stuff the chicken with a third of the mixture.
— Put the chicken in a cooking bag with the water and cook at 100% for 5 minutes; reduce the power level to 70% and continue to cook for 15 minutes.
— Cook the carrots and the strips of turnip at 100% for 5 minutes.
— Stuff the cabbage leaves with the remaining stuffing.
— Arrange the chicken in a casserole with its cooking liquid, the stuffed cabbage leaves and the vegetables.
— Season, cover and cook at 70% for 25 minutes.
— Allow to stand for 10 minutes before serving.

Put the chicken in a cooking bag and close the bag according to the instructions on page 21. Place in a cooking dish.

Cook the carrots and the strips of turnip in a separate casserole.

Remove the chicken and the liquid from the bag and put them into a casserole dish. Add the cooked vegetables and continue to cook.

Chicken à la King

Level of Difficulty	
Preparation Time	20 min
Cost per Serving	$
Number of Servings	6
Nutritional Value	486 calories 42.1 g protein 2.4 mg iron
Food Exchanges	4 oz meat 1/2 milk exchange 1 vegetable exchange 3 fat exchanges
Cooking Time	10 min
Standing Time	None
Power Level	100%, 70%
Write Your Cooking Time Here	

Ingredients
750 mL (3 cups) cooked chicken, diced
75 mL (1/3 cup) butter
1/2 onion, thinly sliced
75 mL (1/3 cup) celery, finely chopped
75 mL (1/3 cup) flour
250 mL (1 cup) chicken stock
250 mL (1 cup) milk
125 mL (1/2 cup) 18% cream
1 mL (1/4 teaspoon) dry mustard
2 mL (1/2 teaspoon) Worcestershire sauce
125 mL (1/2 cup) cooked carrots, sliced
75 mL (1/3 cup) green peas, frozen

Method
— Melt the butter at 100% for 1 minute.
— Add the onion and celery and cook at 100% for 2 minutes.
— Stir in the flour and mix well.
— Add the chicken stock and the milk, stir and cook at 100% until the sauce thickens, stirring every 2 minutes.
— Add the cream, dry mustard, Worcestershire sauce, and mix in the chicken, cooked carrots and peas. Heat at 70% for 4 minutes, stirring halfway through the cooking time.
— Serve over rice or noodles or in hot vol-au-vent cases.

Melt 75 mL (1/3 cup) butter in a bowl. Add the onion and celery and cook at 100% for 2 minutes.

Stir in the flour, using a whisk, and beat until smooth.

Continue beating as you add the chicken stock and milk.

Chicken and Broccoli Quiche

Level of Difficulty	
Preparation Time	30 min
Cost per Serving	$
Number of Servings	6
Nutritional Value	491 calories 21.2 g protein 2.3 mg iron
Food Exchanges	3 oz meat 2 vegetable exchanges 1 bread exchange 3 fat exchanges
Cooking Time	20 min
Standing Time	10 min
Power Level	70%, 100%, 50%
Write Your Cooking Time Here	

Ingredients

Pastry:
500 mL (2 cups) wholewheat flour
125 mL (1/2 cup) shortening
2 mL (1/2 teaspoon) salt
45 mL (3 tablespoons) cold water
2 mL (1/2 teaspoon) poultry seasoning

Filling:
250 mL (1 cup) cooked chicken, diced
30 mL (2 tablespoons) butter
125 mL (1/2 cup) almonds, sliced
3 eggs, lightly beaten
125 mL (1/2 cup) 18% cream
1 284 mL (10 oz) package chopped broccoli, defrosted
250 mL (1 cup) Swiss cheese, grated
30 mL (2 tablespoons) flour
2 mL (1/2 teaspoon) salt
pinch pepper

Method

Pastry:
— Make the pastry in the usual way and work into a single ball.
— Roll out the pastry and line a 22 cm (9 inch) pie plate.
— Prick the pastry with a fork.
— Cook at 70% for 6 minutes or until the pastry is crisp, turning the plate halfway through the cooking time. Set aside.

Filling:
— Melt the butter, add the almonds and cook at 100% for 2 to 3 minutes to brown them.
— Mix the eggs and cream, add the remaining ingredients and pour the mixture into the cooked pastry shell.
— Cook at 50% for 8 minutes, turning the plate halfway through the cooking time.

- Turn the plate again and continue to cook at 50% until a slight froth appears on the surface of the quiche.
- Garnish with the roasted almonds, cover and allow to stand for 10 minutes before serving.

Roll out the pastry and arrange it in a pie plate. Prick the bottom and sides with a fork.

Combine the ingredients for the filling, put into the cooked pastry shell and cook.

Chicken Omelette

Level of Difficulty	
Preparation Time	20 min
Cost per Serving	$
Number of Servings	4
Nutritional Value	366 calories 35.8 g protein 3.9 mg iron
Food Exchanges	4 oz meat 2 vegetable exchanges
Cooking Time	18 min
Standing Time	3 min
Power Level	100%, 70%
Write Your Cooking Time Here	

Ingredients
1 whole chicken breast, cooked and diced
30 mL (2 tablespoons) butter
50 mL (1/4 cup) zucchini, diced
250 mL (1 cup) broccoli, cut into small pieces
125 mL (1/2 cup) mushrooms, sliced
30 mL (2 tablespoons) flour
250 mL (1 cup) chicken stock
4 egg yolks, beaten
4 egg whites
50 mL (1/4 cup) milk

Method
— Melt the butter at 100% for 45 seconds, add the diced zucchini and broccoli and cook at 100% for 3 to 4 minutes.
— Add the chicken and cook at 70% for 6 to 7 minutes, stir in the mushrooms and continue to cook at 70% for 2 minutes.
— Add the flour and mix well, add the chicken stock and cook at 100% until the mixture thickens, stirring every 2 minutes. Cover and put to one side.
— Beat the egg whites until they are stiff and add the yolks and the milk.
— Stir lightly with a fork just 2 or 3 times.
— Pour the egg mixture into a large pie plate and cook uncovered at 70% for 3 to 4 minutes until it thickens, stirring halfway through the cooking time.
— Cover, let stand for 3 minutes, spread the chicken and vegetable mixture over the omelette and fold.

88

Melt the butter in a dish and cook the zucchini, broccoli and chicken.

Pour the egg and milk mixture into a pie plate. Stir the mixture with a fork to ensure even cooking.

Spread the chicken and cooked vegetable mixture evenly over the omelette and fold.

Cabbage Leaves Stuffed with Chicken

Level of Difficulty	🍴
Preparation Time	15 min
Cost per Serving	**S**
Number of Servings	4
Nutritional Value	249 calories 31 g protein 2.5 mg iron
Food Exchanges	3 oz meat 1/2 fruit exchange
Cooking Time	7 min
Standing Time	None
Power Level	100%, 90%
Write Your Cooking Time Here	

Ingredients
360 g (12 oz) cooked chicken, diced
4 large cabbage leaves, cooked
1 398 mL (14 oz) can crushed pineapple, drained
4 green onions, chopped
1 green pepper, chopped
2 mL (1/2 teaspoon) ginger, chopped
45 mL (3 tablespoons) sunflower seeds

Method
— Combine the pineapple, green onions, green pepper and ginger.
— Cook at 100% for 3 minutes or until the vegetables are tender.
— Add the diced chicken and the sunflower seeds and mix well.
— Spoon a portion of the mixture onto the center of each cabbage leaf.
— Fold up the cabbage leaves, secure with toothpicks, cover and cook at 90% for 3 to 4 minutes.
— Serve with rice and top with a sweet and sour sauce.

Assemble all the ingredients for this quick and simple recipe.

Remove the cabbage leaves and stuff them with the mixture of pineapple, vegetables, chicken and sunflower seeds.

Fold up the stuffed cabbage leaves and secure them with toothpicks so that they remain closed during cooking.

Arrange the cabbage leaves in the bottom of a shallow casserole dish, cover and cook for 3 to 4 minutes.

Fettuccine Verde

Level of Difficulty	🍴
Preparation Time	15 min
Cost per Serving	$
Number of Servings	4
Nutritional Value	501 calories 26.1 g protein 1.9 mg iron
Food Exchanges	3 oz meat 2 bread exchanges 1 vegetable exchange 1 fat exchange
Cooking Time	32 min
Standing Time	3 min
Power Level	100%, 70%
Write Your Cooking Time Here	

Assemble the ingredients for this delicious recipe, which will delight lovers of Italian food.

Ingredients
250 mL (1 cup) cooked chicken, diced
225 g (1/2 lb) green fettuccine
5 slices bacon
1 small onion, chopped
1 stick celery, chopped
1 leek, sliced
30 mL (2 tablespoons) flour
30 mL (2 tablespoons) butter
625 mL (2-1/2 cups) milk
garlic pepper
pepper
Parmesan cheese, grated
parsley

Method
— Cook the fettuccine in the required amount of boiling water for 12 minutes at 100%. Stir every 3 minutes.
— Arrange the bacon on a rack, cook at 100% for 5 minutes and crumble.
— Cook the vegetables at 100% for 4 minutes. Set aside.
— Mix the flour and butter, add the milk and cook at 100% for 6 minutes, stirring every 2 minutes.
— Add the chicken, bacon and vegetables to the sauce, season and mix well.
— Arrange the fettuccine in the bottom of a casserole dish and pour the sauce over it.
— Sprinkle with Parmesan cheese and parsley and cook at 70% for 5 to 6 minutes.
— Cover and let stand for 3 minutes before serving.

Chicken Cacciatore

Level of Difficulty	🍴
Preparation Time	20 min
Cost per Serving	$ $
Number of Servings	4
Nutritional Value	443 calories 36.3 g protein 3.1 mg iron
Food Exchanges	4 oz meat 3 vegetable exchanges 2 fat exchanges
Cooking Time	18 min
Standing Time	5 min
Power Level	100%, 70%
Write Your Cooking Time Here	

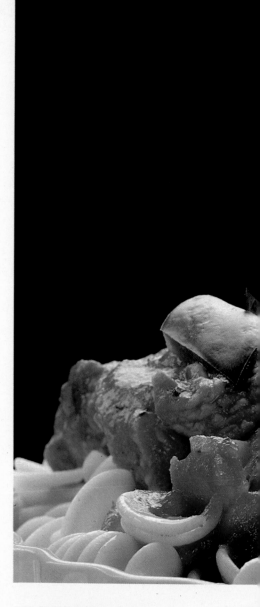

Ingredients
2 whole chicken breasts
30 mL (2 tablespoons) butter
1 onion, diced
50 mL (1/4 cup) mushrooms, sliced
125 mL (1/2 cup) green pepper, diced
1 clove garlic, chopped
1 398 mL (14 oz) can Italian-style tomato sauce
50 mL (1/4 cup) Parmesan cheese, grated

Method
— Cut the breasts in half and bone them. Set aside.
— Melt the butter at 100% for 40 seconds, add the onion, mushrooms, green pepper and garlic and cook at 100% for 3 to 4 minutes. Stir in the tomato sauce.
— Arrange the breasts in the bottom of a casserole dish and cover them with the vegetables and the sauce.
— Cover and cook at 70% for 7 minutes.
— Give the dish a half-turn, rearrange the breasts and baste them with the sauce.
— Cover and cook at 70% for 7 minutes or until the breasts are done.
— Sprinkle with Parmesan cheese, cover and let stand for 5 minutes before serving on a bed of pasta.

MICROTIPS
To Bake Tender Chicken

Chicken cooked in the microwave may sometimes be less tender than when it is cooked in a conventional oven. This may be due to overcooking. It is very important to cook the chicken only as long as indicated. The chicken can be marinated in a teriyaki sauce or other marinade prior to cooking to make it more tender.

MICROTIPS

Defrosting Chicken Legs

Frozen legs bought at the supermarket frequently come stuck together in a single block, making it impossible to separate them before thawing. In such cases, put them on a bacon rack in the microwave oven at the appropriate power level for defrosting. After 6 to 8 minutes, check to see whether they are sufficiently thawed to be separated. If not, continue to check every 2 minutes until they are.

Arrange the legs in a circle, taking care to place the thicker parts toward the outside of the dish. Divide the total time they require in the microwave into periods of equal length and allow for standing times of a quarter of the total defrosting time between each.

Halfway through the defrosting process, give the dish a half-turn so as to ensure even defrosting. Once the defrosting time is up, take the legs out of the oven and allow them to stand for 10 minutes. Rinse in cold water and pat dry before cooking.

Couscous with Chicken and Shrimp

Level of Difficulty	¶¶¶
Preparation Time	30 min
Cost per Serving	$ $
Number of Servings	8
Nutritional Value	299 calories 37.9 g protein 2.7 mg iron
Food Exchanges	3 oz meat 2 vegetable exchanges 1/2 bread exchange
Cooking Time	32-35 min
Standing Time	5 min
Power Level	100%, 70%
Write Your Cooking Time Here	

Ingredients
250 mL (1 cup) couscous
500 mL (2 cups) cold salted water
1.3 kg (3 lb) chicken pieces, skin removed
225 g (1/2 lb) small shrimps, peeled
125 mL (1/2 cup) red pepper, cut into strips
1 medium onion, chopped
1 540 mL (19 oz) can tomatoes
175 mL (3/4 cup) chicken stock
1 284 mL (10 oz) can cut asparagus

Method
— Soak the couscous in the cold water for 15 minutes, stirring every 5 minutes.
— To cook, put the couscous in a sieve with a fine mesh and place in a casserole dish containing a little boiling water.
— Cover with plastic wrap and cook at 100% for 6 to 8 minutes, turning the sieve halfway through the cooking time.
— Combine the peppers and the onion and cook at 100% for 3 to 4 minutes.
— Add the tomatoes and the chicken stock, and pour the mixture into a casserole dish containing the chicken, shrimps and asparagus.
— Cover and cook at 70% for 10 minutes. Give the dish a half-turn and cook at 70% for a further 12 minutes, or until all the ingredients are done.
— Leave the cover on and let stand for 5 minutes before serving with the cooked couscous.

Entertaining

Menu:
Vegetable Soup
Stuffed Turkey
Cranberry and Pear Sauce
Strawberry Sorbet

Why wait for Christmas or Easter to enjoy turkey when it is available all year round? The menu we offer for entertaining features stuffed turkey as the entrée—no better fare could conclude a cook book on poultry.

Turkey became an instant classic when it was introduced in England in the seventeenth century, and it continues to delight lovers of fine food in the western world. It is usually served with another New World classic: cranberry sauce. However, we have chosen to moderate the rather acid flavor of cranberries by mixing them with pears, a combination that we are sure you will find very successful. This meal can be prepared quite quickly and the results should both surprise and delight you.

A first course of vegetable soup will keep the heartiest eaters happy without spoiling lesser appetites. The dessert should be light; we suggest a delicate strawberry sorbet, which is both colorful and fresh tasting.

From the Recipe to Your Table

Planning a meal for a number of friends or relatives is hard work and takes organization. Cooking a complete meal in the microwave oven must be planned ahead in the same way as a meal cooked in a conventional oven. Only the cooking and reheating times vary.

24 hours before the meal:
— Prepare the cranberry and pear sauce.

8 hours before the meal:
— Make the strawberry sorbet and prepare the stuffing.

4 hours before the meal:
— Make the soup.

3 hours before the meal:
— Stuff, prepare and cook the turkey.

20 minutes before the meal:
— Reheat the soup at 90% for 10 to 15 minutes, stirring once halfway through the reheating time.

NOTE: The choice of vegetables to accompany the meal is up to you. However, we suggest a macédoine (a combination of diced vegetables) to add both taste and color. It is a good idea to cook the vegetables in advance and reheat them a few minutes before serving.

Vegetable Soup

Ingredients
1.5 L (6 cups) beef stock
4 carrots, diced
250 mL (1 cup) turnip, diced
4 leeks, sliced
1 onion, quartered
3 sticks celery, diced
2 red peppers, diced
2 green peppers, diced
1 796 mL (28 oz) can
tomatoes

Method
— Cook the carrots and
turnip in as little water as
possible, using a covered
dish and cooking at 100%
for 10 minutes.
— Add all the other
ingredients and cook the
soup at 100% for 30
minutes.
— Stir very thoroughly and

continue cooking at 100%
until all the vegetables are
done.

Cranberry and Pear Sauce

Ingredients
500 mL (2 cups) cranberries
250 mL (1 cup) pears, grated
1 clove
pinch allspice
175 mL (3/4 cup) sugar
50 mL (1/4 cup) port
50 mL (1/4 cup) water
15 mL (1 tablespoon) lemon
juice

Method
— Combine all the
ingredients, cover and
cook at 100% for 10
minutes, stirring halfway
through the cooking time.
— Strain and refrigerate.

Stuffed Turkey

Level of Difficulty	(icon)
Preparation Time	30 min
Cost per Serving	S S
Number of Servings	16
Nutritional Value	546 calories 76.7 g protein 4.9 mg iron
Food Exchanges	6 oz meat
Cooking Time	29 min/kg (13 min/lb)
Standing Time	10 min
Power Level	100%, 70%
Write Your Cooking Time Here	(pencil icon)

Ingredients

Stuffing:
500 mL (2 cups) rice, cooked
450 g (1 lb) lean ground beef
50 mL (1/4 cup) onion,
finely chopped
250 mL (1 cup) celery,
chopped
45 mL (3 tablespoons) butter
pepper
savory
poultry seasoning

Turkey:
1 turkey, 5 to 6 kg (12 lb)
lemon juice
poultry seasoning
pepper
paprika
prepared stuffing
cranberry and pear sauce

Method

Stuffing:
— Brown the onion and the celery in the butter by cooking at 100% for 2 to 4 minutes, add the ground beef and continue to cook at 100% for 4 to 5 minutes, stirring twice.
— Stir in the cooked rice and season to taste.

Turkey:
— Remove the giblets and wash the turkey inside and out. Pat dry.
— Brush the turkey with a mixture of the lemon juice and seasoning.
— Fill the turkey with the prepared stuffing. Close the bird either by sewing it or by putting a piece of bread in the opening to keep the stuffing in place.
— Put the turkey in a cooking bag and place on a microwave-safe dish.
— Cook at 70% for about 29 minutes/kg (13 minutes/lb), turning the turkey over and giving the dish a half-turn twice during cooking.
— Let the turkey stand for 10 minutes.
— Serve with cranberry and pear sauce.

Strawberry Sorbet

Ingredients
175 mL (3/4 cup) sugar
500 mL (2 cups) water
50 mL (1/4 cup) honey
250 mL (1 cup) strawberries, crushed
15 mL (1 tablespoon) lemon juice

Method
— Combine the sugar, water and honey and heat at 100% until the mixture boils.
— Continue to cook until the mixture becomes syrupy, stirring every 2 minutes.
— Allow to stand for 10 minutes, add the strawberries and the lemon juice and mix.
— Freeze for 1 to 2 hours, stirring every 10 minutes to prevent ice crystals from forming.

Flavor Variations for Stuffing

Cooking not only allows you to experiment—it encourages you to do so. For instance, people in the food industry organize international competitions from time to time and award prizes for the best new ideas. Although your experiments may not be on the level of those of a master chef, you can still add a personal touch to basic recipes to enhance the food you serve and, in so doing, both surprise and delight your guests. For this reason, we have decided not to give precise recipes for stuffing here but rather to offer suggestions for ways of adapting stuffing ingredients to suit your own personal taste preferences.

One classic turkey stuffing is made from croûtons. First, cut dry bread into cubes and then fry them in butter. Add any other ingredients and seasonings that go well with turkey, e.g. celery, garlic, parsley and fines herbes. Finally, add the chopped cooked giblets.

For a rather different flavor, add cooked sausage meat seasoned with a little garlic, pepper and nutmeg to the chopped, cooked giblets. Then mix these ingredients with vegetables or croûtons.

If you wish to add a little color to your stuffing, include vegetables in the mixture. For example, spinach is one vegetable that is frequently used. Blanch the vegetables you have chosen, drain them thoroughly, chop and mix them with the cooked giblets. The result will be both delicious and different.

MICROTIPS

Testing for Doneness
To test whether or not a turkey is done before you leave it to stand, use the following method. Insert a meat thermometer into the meat between the thigh and the breast, turn it 2 or 3 times and wait 1 minute. The temperature should reach 85° C (185° F). If it does not reach this temperature, remove the thermometer and continue to cook.

Warning. Never use a conventional meat thermometer in a microwave oven while the oven is on. Instead, use a special microwave-safe thermometer and follow the manufacturer's instructions carefully.

Poultry Terminology

Aromatic: Plant, leaf or herb with a strong and distinctive aroma, used to add a pleasant, subtle taste to dishes.

Ex.: saffron, chevril, tarragon, bay leaf, thyme.

Béchamel: A white sauce made with milk and a roux (see separate entry). Its consistency can vary to suit its particular use. It is easy to make and goes well with poultry.

Bouquet garni: Herbs and aromatics tied between two small sticks of celery or sprigs of parsley, used for flavoring certain dishes (soups, stews, etc.).

Braise: A method of cooking in which poultry or meat is gently simmered over a long period of time in a flavored liquid, but less than that used in stewing.

Breastbone: The ridge of bone distinguishable on the front of all types of poultry. The breast meat is attached to this bone.

Chicken stock: A liquid flavored with chicken, vegetables and seasoning as a result of a very long, slow simmering process.

Chive: A small green onion. All parts are edible.

Croquettes: Small round or oval patties usually made with chopped or minced cooked meat, fish or poultry, vegetables and seasoning. They are crumb coated and baked or deep fat fried.

Escallop: A thin slice of boneless meat (in poultry, usually cut from the breast of turkey) that is usually crumb coated.

Garnish: Usually made from one or more types of vegetables, a garnish is used to decorate a dish and to make it more substantial.

Giblets: Edible innards of a bird, including the liver, heart, gizzard and kidneys.

Gizzard: Part of the digestive tract of a fowl. It is used in stuffing or to make stock.

Jointing poultry: Cutting poultry into serving pieces.

Macédoine:	A combination of diced vegetables.
Oysters:	The delicate wedges of flesh that adjoin the parson's nose and extend into the hollow on each side of the backbone of chicken or turkey.
Parson's nose:	The tail of a bird. The two wedges of meat adjoining the parson's nose on the rump, known as the oysters, are often overlooked.
Pilaf:	A rice dish made with meat and vegetables as well.
Roulade:	A thin slice of boneless meat or poultry spread with a savory filling, rolled up and secured with a toothpick.
Roux:	A mixture of flour and butter that is cooked and used to thicken sauces.
Stuffing:	A mixture of finely chopped ingredients with seasoning used for poultry, vegetables, etc.
Truss:	To secure, by sewing or tying, the legs and wings of a bird so that it will not lose its shape during cooking.
Wishbone:	A V-shaped bone that joins the breastbone to the shoulder.

Culinary Terms

Have you ever been given a menu and found that you were unable to understand many of the words? Not only are there a number of culinary terms that are rather obscure but there are many ways to cook chicken that have a special term to describe them. Here is a short glossary of terms that may help you.

à la bonne femme: with white wine, onions, bacon and potatoes as main ingredients.

à la livournaise: with oil, vinegar, pepper and nutmeg as main ingredients.

à la marseillaise: with garlic, green peppers, tomatoes and lemon juice as main ingredients.

à la niçoise: with garlic, tomatoes, anchovies and black olives as main ingredients.

à la printanière: with a veal-based velouté and fines herbes as main ingredients.

à la reine: supreme sauce (a chicken-based velouté sauce) mixed with whipped cream.

chasseur: with mushrooms, tomatoes and white wine as main ingredients.

Garibaldi: with mustard, garlic, pepper and cayenne as main ingredients.

marengo: a *chasseur* sauce to which garlic is added.

Polignac: a white wine sauce with added cream, served with julienned mushrooms.

soubise: with onions, pepper and cayenne in a béchamel sauce enriched with cream.

Conversion Chart

**Conversion Chart for the
Main Measures Used in
Cooking**

Volume
1 teaspoon............ 5 mL
1 tablespoon......... 15 mL

1 quart (4 cups)....... 1 litre
1 pint (2 cups)....... 500 mL
1/2 cup............ 125 mL
1/4 cup............ 50 mL

Weight
2.2 lb......... 1 kg (1000 g)
1.1 lb............... 500 g
0.5 lb............... 225 g
0.25 lb............. 115 g

1 oz................. 30 g

**Metric Equivalents
for Cooking
Temperatures**

49°C	120°F	120°C	250°F
54°C	130°F	135°C	275°F
60°C	140°F	150°C	300°F
66°C	150°F	160°C	325°F
71°C	160°F	180°C	350°F
77°C	170°F	190°C	375°F
82°C	180°F	200°C	400°F
93°C	200°F	220°C	425°F
107°C	225°F	230°C	450°F

Readers will note that, in the recipes, we give 250 mL as the equivalent for 1 cup and 450 g as the equivalent for 1 lb and that fractions of these measurements are even less mathematically accurate. The reason for this is that mathematically accurate conversions are just not practical in cooking. Your kitchen scales are simply not accurate enough to weigh 454 g—the true equivalent of 1 lb—and it would be a waste of time to try. The conversions given in this series, therefore, necessarily represent approximate equivalents, but they will still give excellent results in the kitchen. No problems should be encountered if you adhere to either metric or imperial measurements throughout a recipe.

Index

MICROTIPS